# PERFECTION

# PERFECTION

## The Abandoned Key

**Richard P. Kuehn**



ELM HILL

A Division of
HarperCollins Christian Publishing

www.elmhillbooks.com

**Perfection**
**The Abandoned Key**



Published in Nashville, Tennessee, by Elm Hill, an imprint of Thomas Nelson. Elm Hill and Thomas Nelson are registered trademarks of HarperCollins Christian Publishing, Inc.

Elm Hill titles may be purchased in bulk for educational, business, fund-raising, or sales promotional use. For information, please e-mail SpecialMarkets@ThomasNelson.com.



**Library of Congress Cataloging-in-Publication Data**

Library of Congress Control Number: 2018930964

ISBN 978-1-595543530 (Paperback)
ISBN 978-1-595556141 (Hardbound)
ISBN 978-1-595544025 (eBook)

# Dedication

To all the saints who have proclaimed God's righteousness and have heeded his call to walk as he walked.

# ACKNOWLEDGMENTS

First, I thank my Lord Jesus Christ and his Holy Spirit for his wisdom, inspiration, patience, and love. Without him, none of this would have been possible or worth a moment's consideration.

Several others have read and made suggestions for this book. To all of them, I give my heartfelt thanks. My special gratitude goes to my faithful, loving, and patient wife, Jackie, who has blessed me greatly throughout my work. I also want to thank Mr. Gordon Palzer for reviewing my grammar and Mrs. Rizza Malong for her thoughtful suggestions and organizational skills. This book also reflects the mentoring of my faithful friends Arlo Scheff and Elmond Kanne, who wrote me many letters of instruction, exhortation, and correction over the years.

Many also have labored over the initial formatting and production issues of this book. Among them are my Filipino churchmates James Manaois, Febie Aryo, and Jhobelle Gonzales, who contributed their artistic, computer, and layout skills to the original work. Now back in the States, I am grateful to the publishing staff at Elm Tree for their diligent efforts in the myriad details of producing this book.

# Table of Contents

# PREFACE

Beloved, I am well aware of Solomon's admonition that "of making many books there is no end, and much study is wearisome to the flesh" (Ecclesiastes 12:12, KJV). Nevertheless, as I have studied the Scriptures over and over again, as I have pondered God's lament over his people being destroyed for lack of knowledge (Hosea 4:6), as I have observed the ravages of sin in the church, and the church becoming more and more irrelevant in families, workplaces, and society, I have become increasingly convinced that another apologetic for Christian perfection is both warranted and necessary. In fact, it is burning in my mind, soul, and spirit. The church simply cannot afford to be regulated to the likes of a service club, a support group, or a prosperity pump. Neither can it afford to ignore the 50 percent of the gospel that empowers the church to be both relevant and powerful. It must regain the significance and position in the kingdom of God, which our Lord Jesus has predestined it to occupy. As the body of Jesus Christ, it must reflect the character of its Founder, and it must bring healing, truth, holiness, righteousness, morality, and true prosperity back to the society it serves. Instead of watching love grow cold through the rise of divorce, drug abuse, child abuse, poverty, wars, oppression, hatred, and strife, the church must be the shining light of hope and the seat of wisdom and righteousness. It must purvey unsullied the gifts and the fruits of the Holy Spirit. It must bring love, joy, peace, patience, kindness, goodness, faithfulness, gentleness, and self-control back to a world starving for these genuine fruits of God. In short, it must become the solution to the world's ills that God intended and predestined it to be.

How is it going to accomplish such a task? It has taken two thousand years for the church to get fragmented and weak. What can possibly repair the breaches, restore the foundations, renovate the interior, and rejuvenate the flock? The answer is profoundly simple: return to our roots.

Jesus said, "I am the vine, you are the branches. He who abides in Me, and I in him, bears much fruit; *for without Me you can do nothing*" (John 15:5, NKJV; italics mine). If we can get sweetly and powerfully reconnected to the Vine, if we will live in him and he in us, our worldviews will change, and we will turn the world upside down for good even as the early church did.

However, many Christians today are operating at 50 percent or less of the whole gospel message—that is, they are very content to be "saved." They have either "said the prayer" or have "been confirmed" or have "been baptized" into a local church or denomination, but they have no concept of what they have been saved from or the meaning of being conformed to the image of Christ. They are happy knowing that Christ died for them, redeemed them, atoned for them, justified them, and gave them eternal life in the hereafter. These are exceedingly great blessings and a cause for praise and thanksgiving, to be sure!

The problem, however, is that all of these are self-centered blessings: things we *get* from God. They are called God's gift of grace to mankind. Frequently they are either consciously or subconsciously used as an insurance policy for salvation. What do I mean? I mean many people want to know what the bottom-line payment is to obtain salvation and eternal life from God. They assume this payment has been made entirely by Christ and that no behavior modification is either expected or necessary. They usually base this on Ephesians 2:8 and 9. They forget the following verse 10. They bristle at anyone who would suggest that godly behavior, behavior conformed to the biblical standards of righteousness and justice, might be necessary for salvation. They call this "works" righteousness and dismiss the idea as the musings of a Jesus freak, a Bible thumper, an uptight conservative, or some similar derogatory epithet designed to disarm or disgrace anyone holding such pedestrian or old-fashioned ideas.

The problem is that Jesus makes some very specific requirements for entering heaven, which are not popular or even understood or taught today. Consider the following:

> For I say to you, that unless your righteousness exceeds the righteousness of the scribes and Pharisees, you will by no means enter the kingdom of heaven.
>
> MATTHEW 5:20 (NKJV)

> Not everyone who says to Me, "Lord, Lord," shall enter the kingdom of heaven, *but he who does the will of My Father* in heaven. Many will say to Me in that day, "Lord, Lord, have we not prophesied in Your name, cast out demons in Your name, and done many wonders in Your name?" And then I will declare to them, "I never knew you; depart from Me, you who practice lawlessness!"
>
> MATTHEW 7:21–23 (NKJV, ITALICS MINE)

Jesus also makes the following statements about his expectations for all who do follow him:

> But I say to you, love your enemies, bless those who curse you, do good to those who hate you, and pray for those who spitefully use you and persecute you.
>
> MATTHEW 5:44 (NKJV)

> Therefore you shall be perfect, just as your Father in heaven is perfect.
>
> MATTHEW 5:48 (NKJV)

> A new commandment I give to you, that you love one another; as I have loved you, that you also love one another. By this all will know that you are My disciples, if you have love for one another.
>
> JOHN 13:34–35 (NKJV)

For clarity of these commands by Jesus Christ in the gospels, at least two more by the Holy Spirit through the apostles Paul and John must be added:

> Pursue peace with all people, and holiness, without which no one will see the Lord:
>
> HEBREWS 12:14 (NKJV)

> He who sins is of the devil, for the devil has sinned from the beginning. For this purpose the Son of God was manifested, that He might destroy the works of the devil. Whoever has been born of God does not sin, for His seed remains in him; *and he cannot sin*, because he has been born of God.
>
> 1 JOHN 3:8–9 (NKJV, ITALICS MINE)

When I first considered these texts together, I was both amazed and not a little concerned. The implications were staggering. Why had no one spoken about these issues before in church? Why did no one else seem to be bothered by these commands and teachings?

At first, I assumed that there must be some way of understanding these, which did not require me to obey what seemed to be unreasonable, if not impossible, commands by the Lord I loved. In the seminary, I even examined 1 John 3:9 in the original Greek to see if there was some way around the clear meaning. However, the more I studied, the more convinced I became that John, by the

Spirit, was serious and that God had a New Testament standard for his children in Christ, which was much higher than the standards he had for the Jews in the Old Testament. And from that time on, I have sought through prayer and meditation and study of the scriptures to understand not man's perspective but God's in regard to his call for his children to be perfect, having victory both over sin and the sinful nature.

Now I know that the knee-jerk reaction to a call to perfection is "C'mon, nobody's perfect." We assume that everyone will agree with that. Most of us know that scriptures say that all have sinned and fallen short of the glory of God, and that there is none righteous, no, not one (Romans 3:10–12, 23, etc.). Knowing, therefore, that we have a sinful nature, that the spirit is willing but the flesh is weak, and that nobody else thinks that perfection is attainable in this side of heaven, we just assume that everything is okay and that all of us who go to church and believe in Jesus will go to heaven. We assume that since we have said the prayer or been baptized as an infant or speak in tongues that we have paid the price necessary to obtain an insurance policy granting us an immediate access to heaven upon completion of the earthly portion of our life. We have assurance of our salvation. Our pastors or priests have given us these assurances, and we have not felt it necessary to examine the scriptures to see if what they have said is the whole truth. We assume that they have studied the issue, that their seminaries have clearly taught them, and that they are zealously passing on this information to the flocks. For some reason, we forget God's chastising of the Old Testament wise men for healing the hurt of the daughter of his people slightly by saying, "Peace! Peace!" when there was no peace (Jeremiah 8:6–12). We also forget Jesus' round condemnation of the scribes and Pharisees in Matthew 23 and the large number of heretical teachings that the church has struggled with over the centuries.

Beloved, isn't it just possible that something is missing today?

Does it concern you that the divorce rate in the church is nearly as high as it is in the rest of society,[1] and that many people do not want to become Christians because, as they look at us, they don't see any difference between us and non-Christians? Does it distress you that our daughters are getting pregnant out of wedlock or that they are having abortions? Does it trouble you that pastors and missionaries and leaders in the church are stumbling morally? Does it give you pause when you consider the weakness of the modern church compared to the church of the first and second centuries and that in many places only a few of its members are men? Does it bother you that there is seemingly no fear of God anymore, when the word says that the fear of the Lord is the beginning of knowledge and wisdom? (Proverbs 1:7; Psalms 111:10) Does it vex you that our nation is slowly but systematically removing God from its schools, governmental agencies, and businesses? Does it disturb you that Christianity for many has been relegated to the likes of a service club, a support group, or a purveyor of superstitious beliefs? Does it rankle you that Christianity has been fragmented into dozens of denominations or that it has been boxed into fundamentalists, evangelicals, Catholics, Pentecostals, charismatics, third wave, and the like? All these concern me greatly. No wonder the church has confused many sincere seekers. No wonder it has become an object of ridicule and derision by its detractors.

Beloved, the call today is back to the Holy Spirit-inspired Word of God and for rebirth individually and corporately into the body of Jesus Christ, which is the church (Ephesians 1:22–23, Colossians 1:18, 24), the one true church of which the Bible speaks. It is the time for repentance: repentance from our pride, divisiveness, independence, and rebellion against the expressed Word of God. Our priorities must be reviewed and conformed to his expressed will that we seek first the kingdom of God and his righteousness, remembering that before we can become his friend, we must be his servant (John 15:15). Finally, the call, beloved, is to understand

God's purposes in his Son and in his Spirit so that we can understand our position and potential in him, his kingdom, and his church. When that understanding dawns, then the issue of Christian perfection will seem both logical and natural. Remember, "Wisdom is the principal thing, therefore get wisdom; and with all thy getting, get understanding" (Proverbs 4:7, KJV).

The following chapters, then, are dedicated to examining the purposes of God in Christ, in the Holy Spirit, and in man. As these purposes are clearly understood and applied to the church, I think it will be clear why Christ mandated perfection and how he provided the means for each of us to walk in it. God bless you as you journey into the mind and heart of our Lord Jesus.

# The Purposes of God in Christ

To begin our quest into the mind and heart of God with regard to Jesus the Christ, we must first understand God's purposes in sending his Son to earth. His decision did not proceed from a vacuum. He considered it from the beginning of time. His prophets had spoken in many places concerning his promises of a messiah. But why this great focus on a coming messiah? What was he going to do when he came? What were God's purposes in sending himself as a man? The principal answers to these questions are found in the prophetic word of Zacharias, the father of John the Baptist, before either John or Jesus were born. The definitive text is from Luke and reads as follows:

> Now his father Zacharias was filled with the Holy Spirit, and prophesied, saying: "Blessed is the Lord God of Israel, For He has visited and redeemed His people, And has raised up a horn of salvation for us In the house of His servant David, As He spoke by the mouth of His holy prophets, Who have been since the world began, That we should be saved from our enemies And from the hand of all who hate us, To perform the mercy promised to our fathers And to remember His holy covenant, The oath which He swore to our father Abraham: To grant us that we, Being delivered from the hand of our enemies, Might serve

> Him without fear, In holiness and righteousness before Him all the days of our life."
>
> LUKE 1:67–75 (NKJV)

Let's unpack this prophecy and look at the five main reasons God sent the Messiah, his only begotten Son, to man. As the light of understanding dawns in these areas, so will our love for the Father and the Son grow deeper.

## Visit Mankind

From the above prophesy, we see that the first purpose of God in sending his Son was to personally visit his creation. This was a huge event for mankind. God had not visited earth to live with his people in person since the garden of Eden. In fact, man's sin had so separated him from God (Isaiah 59:2) that God was not willing to speak with him except on specific occasions through his chosen people, and even then only for specific guidance or prophetic reasons. And those theophanies were rare and generally of very short duration. This time he came personally for very specific purposes and remained in man's presence for thirty-three years. It was unique in the history of God's dealings with man. It was the one and only time in history that God's Spirit hovered over a virgin to supernaturally impregnate her with his Son, Immanuel—God with us—as prophesied by the Prophet Isaiah.

But why did he manifest himself in this way and not to another "Moses" on a mount engulfed in lightning and thunder, for example? Why didn't he come by an earthquake and smoke and fire as he had done for the Israelites in the wilderness on Mount Sinai?

Undoubtedly it was because the Jews knew that history, and the results had not been what either God or they had hoped. The people had repeatedly rebelled against his commandments. Again and again they had returned to idols, astrologers, sorcerers, witches, mediums, and the like. The priests had desecrated the sanctuary and prophesied for reward (Zephaniah 3:4; Micah 3:11–12). People had sacrificed their children to Molech in the fire (Leviticus 20:1–4; 2 Kings 23:1–20, esp. 10). There was no fear of God, there was no integrity, and there was no conformity to the statutes and ordinances that God had given for instruction in righteousness. The people whom God had personally chosen to bless, protect, and exemplify godly government and living on earth had failed their mission and brought reproach and scorn on God.

## To Clean House

Because of all these provocations, unmet covenant terms, and unheeded prophetic warnings, God kept his promise and brought the curses of his covenant (Deuteronomy 28:15ff.) upon the tribes of Israel and destroyed or scattered to the winds all but a remnant. The remaining tribes, especially Judah, had not fared much better. And the remnant that remained at the time that the Romans conquered Jerusalem was divided into various sects. Their excesses are portrayed in Matthew 23. It was time for God to intervene personally in history to remove the dross that had accumulated in the writings and actions of his people over the previous millennia. Things were not well with his people at this time, and it was clear that the rest of the world was not going to respect or follow the God of Israel, the creator of the heavens and the earth, if things did not change.

## To Fulfill Prophesy

A second and very simple reason for his personal visit was that he had promised it. Over and over again, details of his visit as the Messiah had been prophesied in the scriptures. There are actually hundreds of such prophesies in the Old Testament—everything from his being born of a virgin (Isaiah 7:14) to his triumphal entry (Zechariah 9:9) and his crucifixion (Isaiah 53; Psalm 22:12–18). And God is faithful in keeping all of his promises, big and small. None of his words falls to the ground. Every detail of Christ's appearance was carefully planned and executed so that even his promise to come out of Egypt was fulfilled (Hosea 11:1; Matthew 2:13–15, 19–21). Consequently, it was imperative that at some point in history he come and fulfill the prophecies of his servants. About 4 BC to AD 29 was that appointed time.

## To Reveal Himself

The third reason for a personal visit was to show mankind the character, humility, love, and power of God who created the universe. He showed the first three of these in the way he dealt with various types and conditions of people in the gospels. He showed the latter in his signs and wonders, which he used to confirm both his word and his power over creation and natural law. Since he was the original means of creation of the universe, this should come as no surprise to us, but rather as a confirmation of the scriptures' proclamation of his godhood and of his creative hand on earth since the very beginning. Note the following:

> In the beginning was the Word, and the Word was with God, and the Word was God. He was in the beginning with God. All things were made through Him, and without Him nothing was made that was made .... And the Word became flesh and dwelt among us, and we

> beheld His glory, the glory as of the only begotten of the Father, full of grace and truth.
>
> John 1:1–3, 14 (NKJV)

> He is the image of the invisible God, the firstborn over all creation. For by Him all things were created that are in heaven and that are on earth, visible and invisible, whether thrones or dominions or principalities or powers. All things were created through Him and for Him. And He is before all things, and in Him all things consist. And He is the head of the body, the church, who is the beginning, the firstborn from the dead, that in all things He may have the preeminence. For it pleased the Father that in Him all the fullness should dwell.
>
> Colossians 1:15–19 (NKJV)

> Has in these last days spoken to us by His Son, whom He has appointed heir of all things, through whom also He made the worlds.
>
> Hebrews 1:2 (NKJV)

> And to make all see what is the fellowship of the mystery, which from the beginning of the ages has been hidden in God who created all things through Jesus Christ.
>
> Ephesians 3:9 (NKJV)

And because he is the creator of the world and the author of all life on earth, one might expect him to have come as a king or a CEO traveling in great style and riches, sleeping in five-star hotels, hobnobbing with the rich and famous and powerful. He certainly had the right to do so, but he did none of these things.

The fact that this almighty creator God decided to enter the arena of mankind through a virgin espoused to a carpenter is a mighty act of humility. That he chose to have a body that Isaiah 53 indicates was quite average—no form or comeliness, no beauty that we should desire him—again indicates his humility and his desire to mix with mankind as an ordinary man. Even his profession as a carpenter was not considered extraordinary in that day. The advantage to God for coming this way is that no one could later complain this to him: "You don't understand. You never had the problems that I had. You were never poor, hungry, or oppressed. You never had to work hard for a living or take responsibility for a family. You never had my temptations," etc.

But the truth is no one can make these allegations because Jesus experienced all of these things. The Bible says that he was tempted in every way that we were yet without sin (Hebrews 4:15). It further asserts that he worked for a living; that he experienced poverty, hunger, and oppression; and that Jesus quite likely did know the issues of heading a family since there is no reference to his stepfather, Joseph, after age twelve. Precisely because he did experience all these things God established him as mankind's good, merciful, wise, loving, and understanding judge (cf. John 5:22, 30).

## To Restore Theocratic Government

A fourth major reason for his visiting his people in person was to restore the theocracy. When God established his first covenant with Israel on Mount Sinai, he was to be their king. Israel had no king during the times of the judges. It was understood that God was their king and that the judges were simply the administrative heads of the people operating under his direction. At the time of Samuel, however, the people cried out for an earthly king like all the other nations had. When they did so, God made a very pointed comment to Samuel: "And the LORD said to Samuel, 'Heed the voice of the people in all that they say to you; for they have not rejected you, but they have rejected Me, that I should not reign over them.'" (1 Samuel 8:7, NKJV)

Therefore, from the time of Saul, the first king of Israel, until the time of the Babylonian captivity, they had various human kings.

By the time of Jesus's birth, what remained of national Israel had no king at all. In fact, it was a small "nation" under the dominion of the Roman Empire. The administrative and religious leadership of the people was vested largely in the Sanhedrin and the high priests. It was at this time that God chose to enter human history to restore his theocracy.

John the Baptist was the first to announce this fact: "Repent; for the kingdom of heaven is at hand" (Matthew 3:2, KJV). Jesus confirmed this statement with his first recorded words in the Gospel of Mark: "The time is fulfilled, and the kingdom of God is at hand. Repent, and believe in the gospel" (Mark 1:15, NKJV).

To further emphasize the importance and significance of these statements, Jesus proclaimed that the very reason that he had been sent to mankind was to preach the kingdom of God! (Luke 4:43) If you've ever wondered about what Jesus preached besides the Sermon on the Mount, you should note that the Word records the following:

> Now it came to pass, afterward, that He went through every city and village, preaching and bringing the glad tidings of the kingdom of God.
>
> Luke 8:1 (NKJV)

It's also instructive to note parenthetically that during the mentoring stage of his disciples, he sent them out do the same:

> Then he called his twelve disciples together and gave them power and authority over all demons, and to cure diseases. He sent them to preach the kingdom of God and to heal the sick.
>
> Luke 9:1–2 (NKJV)

> Jesus said to him, "Let the dead bury their own dead, but you go and preach the kingdom of God."
>
> LUKE 9:60 (NKJV)

But people were confused, especially the scribes and the Pharisees. They looked at Jesus and saw a very ordinary man. He had no political connections. He had no military connections. He didn't even socialize with the religious leaders of his time. How could this be the Messiah? How could this be the one God who would free the people from the Roman Empire and set up the earthly kingdom that the Jews expected? They could not understand his teachings. They did not like his bluntness and frankness. They smarted at his rebukes. They marveled at his miracles, his love for the poor, and his motley followers. It just didn't make sense to them. Ultimately, in frustration and confusion, the scribes and the Pharisees demanded from Jesus when the kingdom of God would come!

Christ's answer to their demands was profound and deserves careful consideration. He said, "The kingdom of God does not come with observation; nor will they say, 'See here!' or 'See there!' For indeed, the kingdom of God is within you" (Luke 17:20–21, NKJV).

To Israel, the greatest surprise of all was that their Messiah had never intended to set up an earthly kingdom as they expected. The kingdom that he came to establish was the kingdom that ruled in men's minds and hearts—not one which, through external laws, forced them into obedience. It was a revolutionary idea. It was a God idea. It was cross-cultural, it was cross-lingual, it was cross-racial, it was transnational, and it was the only kingdom that could bring unity of heart and spirit to a grossly divided and bellicose world. It was a pure stroke of genius, one which even many Christians do not understand today. Many believers think that the kingdom of God will only come at Christ's second coming. But this answer of Christ's clearly states that the kingdom of God is within us. It comes when we invite Jesus Christ, the King of kings and Lord of lords, into our heart. When he comes, the King resides there; and his kingdom is established. It is part of conversion as Paul confirms: "If any man be in Christ he is a new creation, old things have passed away, behold all things have become new" (2 Corinthians 5:17). Our worldview changes, and we see everything differently. We are baptized (washed) and filled with God's Holy Spirit, and we receive at least one gift and all of the fruits of the Spirit. Christ becomes our King, our ruler, our Lord; and we acknowledge that we are sojourners here on earth and that our citizenship is in heaven with Christ. All others around the world who have similarly been converted are our brothers and sisters, a holy priesthood, the temple of the living God (1 Peter 2:5, 9; 1 Corinthians 3:16).

Truly it was the quintessential time to visit his people. He had so many things to do and to share during the visit. And every detail had been planned in advance. Jesus spoke nothing on his own authority, but only said and did what his Father bid him to say and do (John 6:16–18, 8:28–29, 12:49–50). He was obedient to the end, submitting to extreme fasting, the endurance of the temptations of the devil, verbal and physical abuse, and even death on the cross in order to fulfill his Father's will. His visit was the supreme act of love and humility. We really do love him because he first loved us (1 John 4:19).

## Redeem His People

The second specific reason that Zacharias prophetically gives for Christ's coming was to redeem his people. *Redeem* means "to buy back" or "release from bondage." The modern pawnshop provides a good illustration of redemption. When a person needs extra cash, he can take his watch or something of value to a pawnshop and exchange it for the cash he needs. When times get better, he can go to buy back the pawned item for the amount of money he received plus service and interest. When a person buys his pawned item back, it's called redeeming the item. In a similar fashion, when we sin, we pawn our lives to Satan. The problem for man is that he has no way of redeeming, or buying back, his life. It is too stained with sin, too cheap, and devalued. He has neither principle nor interest to satisfy Satan, the pawnshop owner. But because Jesus's life was sinless and perfect, it was like taking a flawless, fifty-carat ruby to buy back a sackful of cut glass! His life was valuable enough to pay for all sinners and to redeem us from the prison of Satan's pawnshop.

### From the Bondage of Sin

In similar fashion, it was necessary that Christ should come to buy back his people from the prison that sin erected. Since every one of us has sinned and fallen short of the glory of God (Romans 3:23), and since the wages of sin is death (Romans 6:23), all of us are or have been on death row. Sin separates us from God and places us in line for judgment. It's a sorry situation for all mankind; and since God is a just God, he has no alternative but to execute the penalty for sin. Satan, the accuser, who was judged by God for his rebellion in heaven (Revelation 12:7–9 and 20:10), would be incensed if God did not carry out justice equally and give us the righteous judgment we deserve too.

The problem was then, and is now, that God did not want to

sentence everybody on earth to the death they deserved (2 Peter 3:9). He has never wanted this. He created man in his own image, and when he was finished with creation, he saw that all he had made was good. He even gave mankind authority on earth to manage and subdue his creation (Genesis 1:26–31). He understood man's potential and desired that man live up to his created capabilities and live in harmony and love with his fellows. Therefore it was necessary for him to come up with a plan that would both fulfill all righteousness and also supernaturally enable man to live a righteous life after his redemption.

## By a Blood Sacrifice

The first part of God's resulting plan of redemption is fairly well known by all Christians. God sent his Son to proclaim the kingdom of God, live a perfect life, and die as a perfect sacrifice for the sins of the world. What is not clearly understood by many Christians and non-Christians alike is why it was necessary that blood be shed. What is this whole business of sacrifice? The answer becomes clear when one studies Leviticus 17:10–11 in conjunction with Hebrews 9:22 and John 6:53–58, 63:

> And whatsoever man there be of the house of Israel, or of the strangers that sojourn among you, that eateth any manner of blood; I will even set my face against that soul that eateth blood, and will cut him off from among his people. For the life of the flesh is in the blood: and I have given it to you upon the altar to make an atonement for your souls: for it is the blood that maketh an atonement for the soul.
>
> Leviticus 17:10–11 (KJV)

> And according to the law almost all things are purified with blood, and without shedding of blood there is no remission.
>
> Hebrews 9:22 (NKJV)

> Then Jesus said to them, "Most assuredly, I say to you, unless you eat the flesh of the Son of Man and drink His blood, you have no life in you. Whoever eats My flesh and drinks My blood has eternal life, and I will raise him up at the last day. For My flesh is food indeed, and My blood is drink indeed. He who eats My flesh and drinks My blood abides in Me, and I in him. As the living Father sent Me, and I live because of the Father, so he who feeds on Me will live because of Me. This is the bread which came down from heaven—not as your fathers ate the manna, and are dead. He who eats this bread will live forever." ... "It is the Spirit who gives life; the flesh profits nothing. The words that I speak to you are spirit, and they are life."
>
> JOHN 6:53–58, 63 (NKJV)

There are two key thoughts to remember from the Leviticus 17 passage above. One is that blood represents the life of an animal, and two is that God has given blood to atone for the sin of a soul. When these are understood, then it becomes clear that all life belongs to God; and, therefore, no one may eat the blood or, spiritually, consume the life of any animal. It belongs to God and must be poured on the ground (Deuteronomy 12:23–27). Further, since the wages of sin is death (Romans 6:23), and since all have sinned (Romans 3:23), there must be a perfect blood sacrifice in order to atone for the souls of mankind. Since Jesus is the sinless Lamb of God, he became the requisite sacrifice for our sins, and his blood the atonement for our souls.

The confusion of the Jews over Jesus's invitation to eat his flesh and blood becomes clearer in light of the above passages. The Jews knew that it was not permitted for them to eat the blood of an animal, much less a human being. Therefore they were offended by Jesus's comments. In fact, many of his disciples deserted him because of these words (cf. John 6:66). But the richness and the beauty of this teaching lies in remembering that the blood spiritually represents the life of the animal and atonement for the soul.

Jesus is hereby exhorting us to take his life and sufferings (his blood and flesh) into us so that we might receive *his life in us* and so that *his blood might atone for our souls.* His command is to be spiritually understood and obeyed, not literally. His words are spirit and truth. Likewise, verse 63 makes it clear that we are not to eat his literal flesh and blood. Jesus himself is eternal life; and when we have him spiritually within us, then we have eternal life. If we do not have him in us, we do not have eternal life (1 John 5:11–12). It is a very rich and deep teaching. More will be said about the subject when we talk about the blood of the new covenant and the mind of Christ.

Since even from the beginning sin required a blood sacrifice (the loss of life), it was necessary that Jesus be our sacrifice. His sinless, perfect life made him the only one who qualified. The Lamb of God had to be without blemish, and blood had to be shed, because without the shedding of blood, there is no remission of sin (Hebrews 9:22).

## To Atone and Justify

Well, what did this redemption accomplish? The theological words are *atonement* and *justification.* Isaiah states plainly that our iniquities have separated us from our God, and our sins have hidden his face from us so that he will not hear us (Isaiah 59:2). There are two great consequences, therefore, of sin. One is that it separates us from God. Quite literally, Adam and Eve were expelled from the garden of Eden, and God no longer walked with them. They were separated from God, as are all of us who have sinned. Furthermore, our sins have hidden God's face from us so that he will not even hear us! Think what that means about our prayers if we willingly engage in sin. Psalm 66:18 says that God will not hear us. Since all of us have sinned and fallen short of the glory of God, it is clear that this puts all of us in a perilous state.

We are separated from God and unable to buy our release from the bondage of our sin.

But when Christ died for us, his blood washed away our sins and restored our relationship with the Father. We were reconciled with God (2 Corinthians 5:18). This supernatural cleansing resulted in what is called "substitutionary atonement," the bringing together of two alienated persons by the satisfactory payment, or redemption, of a third.

Second, this supernatural cleansing and death payment legally left us sinless (justified) in his eyes. At judgment day, Jesus can stand before the Father as our advocate and say, "This person is mine. I paid for his or her sins in full" (1 John 2:2–3 and Romans 5:9).

Truly, redemption was one of God's most well-known and important purposes for sending his son Jesus to earth. Praise God for his beautiful plan of redemption. Thank God that he liberated us from this spiritual prison and separation. And thank Jesus for his willingness to suffer for you and me to accomplish it.

## Save His People

The first two reasons God sent his Son—to visit and to redeem—are vitally important in terms of imparting to us his personal graces and placing us in the position of reconciled children, but it is the third that granted us the ability to follow him in holiness and righteousness. It is only in our salvation that he defeated our real enemies and set us truly free.

The name "Jesus" means "Yahweh saves" or "Savior." The

religious elite of his day misunderstood him because they were looking for a worldly savior, one who would establish an ordinary kingdom, remove the Romans, and put Israel back on the political map of the world. They were confused and perplexed by this powerful carpenter. He didn't look or behave like a savior. His wonder-working powers and his love for the poor and needy were obvious, but the rest just didn't seem to fit. In the end, they blasphemed the Spirit by attributing his work to Satan (Mark 3:29–30) and condemning him as an impostor king.

And while we of the twenty-first century know these things because we have our Bible, it's interesting to consider what many do not know. For example, from what did Jesus save us? Most will say from hell or separation from God or eternal death or the like. The Bible makes it clear, however, that these are secondary effects of our salvation, not the foci of it. The principle strongholds that God attacked and destroyed to save us were Satan, sin, and death. These are the bonds that Jesus was sent to break so that we might be saved from our enemies and restored to God. Let's see how he did it.

## From Their Sin

Macroscopically, sin is the most important of these bonds and often the hardest to break. Nevertheless, when it is broken, the powers of both Satan and death are also neutralized. That is why sin became the number one target of God in Christ. Note what the Bible records of Gabriel's instruction to Joseph about the name and purpose of God's Son to be born of Mary: "And she will bring forth a Son, and you shall call His name JESUS, for He will save His people from their sins" (Matthew 1:21, NKJV).

Note carefully that he was to save us *from* our sins. It does *not* say that he was to save us *in* our sins. There is a difference. I've heard many people say that Jesus died for my past sins, my present sins, and my future sins. And while that may be true in one sense, frequently the person means that since Christ died for him and washed away all his past, present, and future sins, he doesn't need to worry about sinning any more. I even had one prominent Christian tell me on the phone that he sins willfully and it's okay. His eternal security teachings led him to believe that once he is saved, he is always saved. Logically, therefore, he didn't think it mattered now if he sinned willfully or accidentally.

Many people hold similar views in direct opposition to the Word of God. Jesus did not die for our sins so that we could simply go on committing more and more sins with impunity. He did not expect us to sin, claim 1 John 1:9, and sin again. It is not "sin then confess, sin then confess, and sin then confess." Where is the victory in that? Where is the light upon the hill? Where's the bride without blemish? Where is the prophetic word of Zacharias that we "might serve Him without fear, in holiness and righteousness before Him, all the days of our life" in that?

The Bible says that Jesus came to save us from our sins. It further says this:

> For if we sin *willfully* after we have received the knowledge of the truth, there no longer remains a sacrifice for sins, but a certain fearful expectation of judgment, and fiery indignation which will devour the adversaries. Anyone who has rejected Moses' law dies without mercy on the testimony of two or three witnesses. Of how much worse punishment, do you suppose, will he be thought worthy who has trampled the Son of God underfoot, counted the blood of the covenant by which he was sanctified a common thing, and insulted the Spirit of grace? For we know Him who said, "Vengeance is Mine, I will repay," says the Lord. And again, "The LORD will judge His people." It is a fearful thing to fall into the hands of the living God.
>
> Hebrews 10:26–31 (NKJ, italics mine)

It is also instructive to note Numbers 15:22–30 in this regard. Here the Lord specifically states that the Jews could not offer sin sacrifices for any sin that was done deliberately. Anyone who sinned willfully would be cut off from Israel. Apparently that standard has not changed. Jesus came to save us *from* our sins, not *in* them.

## From the Hand of All Who Hate Us

Furthermore, he came to save us from the hand of all who hate us. That is interesting, since at first blush, it doesn't appear that Jesus did this. He certainly didn't save the Jews from the Romans or from any other people who may have hated them. So did he, in fact, save the Jews and us from the hand of all who hate us? Yes, he did! Note this very carefully, *people are not our real enemies.* Paul clearly states this in Ephesians 6:12:

> For we do not wrestle against flesh and blood, but against principalities, against powers, against the rulers of the darkness of this age, against spiritual hosts of wickedness in the heavenly places.
>
> Ephesians 6:12 (NKJV)

Our real enemies, then, are the rulers of the darkness and the spiritual hosts of wickedness. In short, these are Satan and his minions. Why? Because Satan is a liar and the father of lies (John 8:44). His purposes are to steal, kill, and destroy (John 10:10). He has come to steal God's sheep to kill them by sin and to destroy the church, which is the body of Jesus Christ. And Peter warns us very directly as follows: "Be sober, be vigilant; because your adversary the devil walks about like a roaring lion, seeking whom he may devour" (1 Peter 5:8, NKJV).

But how can Satan steal God's sheep (c.f. John 10:10)? Some, in fact, will say this is impossible. They will quote John 10:27–29, and it is indeed a wonderful passage. It assures us that no entity can take us out of the Father's hand. But note what it does *not* say: it does not say that *you* cannot reject God's will and fall away from him—it only says that no one else can take you out of his hand.

Beloved, understand this: Satan does not care how he turns you away from Jesus Christ. His favorite deceptions are the cults and occults. In the area of cults, his favorite ploy is to try to convince people that Jesus is not God, that he is only a man. Note the following:

> Beloved, do not believe every spirit, but test the spirits, whether they are of God; because many false prophets have gone out into the world. By this you know the Spirit of God: Every spirit that confesses that Jesus Christ has come in the flesh [lit. in the Greek "out of the God] is of God, and every spirit that does not confess that Jesus Christ has come in the flesh [lit. "out of the God"] is not of God. And this is the spirit of the Antichrist, which you have heard was coming, and is now already in the world.
>
> 1 JOHN 4:1–3 (NKJV)

There are many cults today whose doctrines hold that Jesus Christ is not God Almighty. Some believe that he's the Son of God, that he is a god, that he is the Messiah, that he is the Christ, etc., but they deny the Trinity and the fact that Jesus is Almighty God. The Scriptures, however, are clear both in the New Testament and the Old Testament that Jesus is Jehovah, God Almighty, the Word of God, the second person of the Trinity, and the manifestation of God in the flesh. Note the following verses:

> Hear, O Israel: The LORD [Jehovah] our God [lit. plural "gods"], the LORD [Jehovah] is one!
>
> DEUTERONOMY 6:4 (NKJV)

In the beginning was the Word, and the Word was with God, and the *Word was God.* He was in the beginning with God.

JOHN 1:1–2 (NKJV, ITALICS MINE)

And the *Word became flesh* and dwelt among us, and we beheld His glory, the glory as of the only begotten of the Father, full of grace and truth.

JOHN 1:14 (NKJV, ITALICS MINE)

But to the Son He says: "Your throne, O God, is forever and ever; A scepter of righteousness is the scepter of Your Kingdom."

HEBREWS 1:8 (NKJV)

Simon Peter, a bondservant and apostle of Jesus Christ, To those who have obtained like precious faith with us by the righteousness of our *God and Savior* Jesus Christ.

2 PETER 1:1 (NKJV, ITALICS MINE)

That Jesus was God and active in the Old Testament is also clear when you compare John 8:58 with Exodus 3:13–15.

Jesus said to them, "Most assuredly, I say to you, before Abraham was, I AM."

JOHN 8:58 (NKJV)

Then Moses said to God, "Indeed, when I come to the children of Israel and say to them, 'The God of your fathers has sent me to you,' and they say to me, 'What is His name?' what shall I say to them?" And God said to Moses, "*I AM WHO I AM.*" And He said, "Thus you shall say to the children of Israel, '*I AM* has sent me to you.'" Moreover God said to Moses, "Thus you shall say to the children of Israel: 'The LORD God of your fathers, the God of Abraham, the God of Isaac, and the

> God of Jacob, has sent me to you. *This is My name forever,* and this is My memorial to all generations.'"
>
> EXODUS 3:13–15 (NKJV, ITALICS MINE)

Clearly Jesus was claiming here to be the very God with whom Moses spoke at the burning bush. But that's not all. Note that the God who spoke to John in the book of Revelation, chapter 1, is the same as the one [God] talking to Isaiah in Isaiah 48. The key is the expression "I am the First, I am also the Last." Compare carefully the following:

> "I am the Alpha and the Omega, the Beginning and the End," says the Lord, "who is and who was and who is to come, *the Almighty.*"... saying, "I am the Alpha and the Omega, *the First and the Last,*" ... "I am He who lives, *and was dead,* and behold, I am alive forevermore. Amen. And I have the keys of Hades and of Death."
>
> REVELATION 1:8, 11, 18 (NKJV, ITALICS MINE)

> Listen to Me, O Jacob, And Israel, My called: *I am He, I am the First, I am also the Last...* Come near to Me, hear this: I have not spoken in secret from the beginning; From the time that it was, I was there. And now the Lord GOD and His Spirit Have [lit. singular in Hebrew: *has*] sent Me.
>
> ISAIAH 48:12, 16 (NKJV, ITALICS MINE)

These verses make it clear that it is the same person, "the First and the Last," who is speaking both in the Revelation and in the Isaiah passages. Further, the context makes it clear that this person is the Lord Jesus (verse 18), that he was sent by the Father and his Spirit (verse 16), and that he is "*the Almighty*" (verse 8). Study these passages well until you understand the full implications of what they say, especially the singular verb in the Isaiah passage.

Satan and his cults would have you believe that Jesus is not

God. But this is not true. It is a lie intended to deceive and steal you away from the true Christ and his salvation. As the quintessential liar and deceiver, Satan is mankind's enemy number one.

A second and far less subtle deception used by Satan is the occult. There are several varieties that he uses around the world, but the two most prevalent are voodoo, in its various forms, and idolatry. Voodoo's practitioners use diverse forms of magic sometimes coded by colors, including black, white, red, yellow, and others. The people who use these forms of magic go by various names, but the most common and generic are witch doctor, medium, warlock, witch, spiritist, necromancer, and the like. There are also those who use fortune-telling (tarot cards, Ouija boards, palm reading, crystals, psychometry, tea leaves, astrology, horoscopes, etc.) that attempt to show Satan's powers and take individuals away from belief in Jesus Christ.

These deceptive influences are not minor or exceptional issues. While my wife Jackie and I were missionaries in the Philippines, we documented more than thirty cults and seventy occultic practices in addition to overt Satanism. Satan has put on a full-court press to distract and discredit true Christianity.

It is not the purpose of this book, however, to explicate the ways Satan and his demons try to take people away from Jesus Christ. Suffice it to say that Satan does have power, and he uses it forcefully to deceive billions of people. But fear not, beloved, we've often seen demons cast out and Satan defeated by the truth and by the name of Jesus Christ. The devil is no match for God. While he and his minions pose the greatest external threat to truth and righteousness in the world, Jesus defeated them all at the cross.

## From the Second Death

The third and last great enemy of man is death (1 Corinthians 15:26). Had Adam and Eve not sinned and rebelled against God's word, they and their progeny could have eaten of the tree of life and lived forever. But because of their disobedience, (1) eternal life in God's presence was taken away from mankind, (2) Adam and Eve were both cursed and removed from the Garden, and (3) death entered the world.

And by *death* Paul does not simply mean *physical death*. All mankind experiences physical death, at least until the return of the Lord. But there is another death that is far more frightening than physical death, and that is what Revelation calls the "second death" or "the lake of fire" (Revelation 20:14–15). Most people know it as the place called hell. And Jesus himself affirms that it is a real place, not some allegorical venue of judgment. According to Revelation, the following will experience this second death:

> But the cowardly, unbelieving, abominable, murderers, sexually immoral, sorcerers, idolaters, and all liars shall have their part in the lake which burns with fire and brimstone, which is the second death.
>
> REVELATION 21:8 (NKJV)

The following verses also give examples of sinful behavior that results in the second death:

> Now the works of the flesh are evident, which are: adultery, fornication, uncleanness, lewdness, idolatry, sorcery, hatred, contentions, jealousies, outbursts of wrath, selfish ambitions, dissensions, heresies, envy, murders, drunkenness, revelries, and the like; of which I tell you beforehand, just as I also told you in time past, that those who practice such things will not inherit the kingdom of God.
>
> GALATIANS 5:19–21 (NKJV)

> But fornication and all uncleanness or covetousness, let it not even be named among you, as is fitting for saints; neither filthiness, nor foolish talking, nor coarse jesting, which are not fitting, but rather giving of thanks. For this you know, that no fornicator, unclean person, nor

> covetous man, who is an idolater, has any inheritance in the kingdom of Christ and God. Let no one deceive you with empty words, for because of these things the wrath of God comes upon the sons of disobedience. Therefore do not be partakers with them. For you were once darkness, but now you are light in the Lord. Walk as children of light.
>
> Ephesians 5:3–8 (NKJV)

> Therefore put to death your members which are on the earth: fornication, uncleanness, passion, evil desire, and covetousness, which is idolatry. Because of these things the wrath of God is coming upon the sons of disobedience, in which you yourselves once walked when you lived in them. But now you yourselves are to put off all these: anger, wrath, malice, blasphemy, filthy language out of your mouth. Do not lie to one another, since you have put off the old man with his deeds.
>
> Colossians 3:5–9 (NKJV)

> Whoever commits sin also commits lawlessness, and sin is lawlessness.
>
> 1 John 3:4 (NKJV)

Since the Bible concludes that all of us have sinned and fallen short of the glory of God, that all of us are guilty of one or more of the sins above, and that the wages of sin is death, then clearly death, the ubiquitous result of sin, is a terrifying enemy of man. Had God not dealt with this enemy through his Son, all mankind would have been doomed to an eternity of torment.

## Summary

To conclude, Jesus was not sent to condemn the world but that the world through him might be saved from our real enemies: Satan, sin, and death, not people. People, even terrorists, merely act on what they believe to be true. That is why the truth is such a key factor in salvation and faith and why Jesus said, "I am the truth" (John 14:6, NKJV). That is also why he sent the Spirit of truth, the Holy Spirit, to help and teach us (John 14:16–17, 26) and why it is the truth that will set us free from the lies, the deceptions, and the bondage of the evil one (John 8:32, 36). Finally, that is why John, through the Spirit, is so delighted by all who walk in the truth (3 John 3–4).

So then, did Jesus actually save us from Satan, sin, and death? Examine the following verses and note that he really did:

> Inasmuch then as the children have partaken of flesh and blood, He Himself likewise shared in the same, that through death He might destroy him who had the power of death, that is, the devil,
>
> HEBREWS 2:14 (NKJV)

> You are of God, little children, and have overcome them, because He who is in you is greater than he who is in the world
>
> 1 JOHN 4:4 (NKJV)

> We know that whoever is born of God does not sin; but he who has been born of God keeps himself, and the wicked one does not touch him.
>
> 1 JOHN 5:18 (NKJV)

> He who sins is of the devil, for the devil has sinned from the beginning. For this purpose the Son of God was manifested, that He might destroy the works of the devil. Whoever has been born of God does not sin, for His seed remains in him; and he cannot sin, because he has been born of God.
>
> 1 JOHN 3:8–9 (NKJV)

> No temptation has overtaken you except such as is common to man; but God is faithful, who will not allow you to be tempted beyond what you are able, but with the temptation will also make the way of escape, that you may be able to bear it.
>
> 1 CORINTHIANS 10:13 (NKJV)

> But has now been revealed by the appearing of our Savior Jesus Christ, who has abolished death and brought life and immortality to light through the gospel.
>
> 2 TIMOTHY 1:10 (NKJV)

Hallelujah! This is really good news. We have an awesome Savior, Jesus Christ, who saved us from our enemies and from the hands of all who hate us. Salvation, then, was the third significant purpose of God in sending his Son to earth.

## Keep His Promises

A fourth specific purpose of Jesus Christ delineated in Zacharias's prophecy of him in Luke 1 is that Jesus would perform the mercy promised to the fathers. God is faithful to his word. He fulfills his prophecies. He keeps his promises. This is a character trait of our righteous and faithful Father. And God made many powerful, specific, and enduring promises to his people. A key factor in his plan to keep these promises is centered in his Son, Jesus Christ. Let's take a look at just a few of these significant pledges in order to understand how important it was for God to send Jesus when he did to personally demonstrate his faithfulness in keeping his covenants with man.

### The Abrahamic Covenant

> Then the Angel of the LORD called to Abraham a second time out of heaven, and said: "By Myself I have sworn, says the LORD, because you have done this thing, and have not withheld your son, your only

> son—blessing I will bless you, and multiplying I will multiply your descendants as the stars of the heaven and as the sand which is on the seashore; and your descendants shall possess the gate of their enemies. In your seed all the nations of the earth shall be blessed, because you have obeyed My voice."
>
> GENESIS 22:15–18 (NKJV)

From the above, it is clear that God made a promise to Abraham long before it was fulfilled. By the time of Christ, the nations of the earth had not yet been blessed by Abraham's seed or their obedience to God. Israel had been hard-hearted and rebellious against God, and after sending prophet after prophet warning Israel to repent and return to him, God finally scattered them around the world. The Israel of Christ's time was a land dominated and occupied by the Roman Empire, and it contained only a remnant of Abraham's physical descendants. It was by no stretch of the imagination a blessing to all the nations of the earth.

But Jesus was a descendant of Abraham, and in him all the nations of the world have been blessed. In fact, the Bible says that Christians are the seed of Abraham. Consider the following verses:

> Just as Abraham "believed God, and it was accounted to him for righteousness." Therefore *know that only those who are of faith are sons of Abraham.* And the Scripture, foreseeing that God would justify the Gentiles by faith, preached the gospel to Abraham beforehand, saying, "In you all the nations shall be blessed." So then those who are of faith are blessed with believing Abraham.
>
> GALATIANS 3:6–9 (NKJV, ITALICS MINE)

> Now to Abraham and his Seed were the promises made. He does not say, "And to seeds," as of many, but as of one, "And to your Seed," who is Christ.
>
> GALATIANS 3:16 (NKJV)

> And if you are Christ's, then you are Abraham's seed, and heirs according to the promise.
>
> Galatians 3:29 (NKJV)

It was therefore necessary that Christ come at this time and in this way in order for God to fulfill his promises to Abraham and to emphasize the importance of faith in the church. God does nothing by accident or coincidence, and he is faithful to his promises. Consequently, all the peoples of the earth have been blessed by Christians, Abraham's spiritual descendants, through the spreading of the gospel of Jesus Christ, the world's Redeemer and Savior.

## The Davidic Covenant

In a similar fashion, God also made a personal promise to David concerning his descendants. Note the following:

> "When your days are fulfilled and you rest with your fathers, I will set up your seed after you, who will come from your body, and I will establish his kingdom. He shall build a house for My name, and I will establish the throne of his kingdom forever. I will be his Father, and he shall be My son. If he commits iniquity, I will chasten him with the rod of men and with the blows of the sons of men. But My mercy shall not depart from him, as I took it from Saul, whom I removed from before you. And your house and your kingdom shall be established forever before you. Your throne shall be established forever."
>
> According to all these words and according to all this vision, so Nathan spoke to David.
>
> 2 Samuel 7:12–17 (NKJV)

Here again it is necessary to understand both the physical and the spiritual significance of the promise. Jesus was a descendant of David physically through Mary (Luke's genealogy). His stepfather, Joseph, was also of the tribe of David (Matthew's genealogy).

Because of this latter circumstance, Joseph and Mary traveled to Bethlehem, the city of David, to be taxed. And it was there that Jesus was born as prophesied in Micah 5:2. Again, every detail is important to God. But that's as far as the physical promise goes.

**Jesus as King of Kings and Lord of Lords**

After carefully establishing the physical lineage of Jesus Christ, it was necessary that the Spirit establish Jesus's royal position in that family. While the gospels record Jesus's teachings on God's kingdom, it is Paul in his first letter to Timothy who clearly reveals his status in it: "He is the King of kings and Lord of lords" (1 Timothy 6:15, NKJV). He is the last and forever King of Israel. God, therefore, kept his covenant with David that he would establish his throne forever through establishing his Son Jesus Christ as David's perpetual successor to the throne of Israel.

Well, if that is the case, how do we non-Jewish believers fit into this promise? Peter addresses this issue in his first letter to the Gentile churches scattered throughout Pontus, Galatia, Cappadocia, Asia, and Bithynia. Here's what he said to them:

> You also, as living stones, are being built up a spiritual house, a holy priesthood, to offer up spiritual sacrifices acceptable to God through Jesus Christ. Therefore it is also contained in the scripture "Behold, I lay in Zion A chief cornerstone, elect, precious, And he who believes on Him will by no means be put to shame." Therefore, to you who believe, He is precious; but to those who are disobedient, "The stone which the builders rejected Has become the chief cornerstone," and "A stone of stumbling And a rock of offense." They stumble, being disobedient to the word, to which they also were appointed. But you are a chosen generation, a royal priesthood, a holy nation, His own special people, that you may proclaim the praises of Him who called you out of darkness into His marvelous light.
>
> 1 PETER 2:5–9 (NKJV)

To this Paul adds the following:

> For *he is not a Jew, which is one outwardly*; neither is that circumcision, which is outward in the flesh: *But he is a Jew, which is one inwardly*; and circumcision is that of the heart, in the spirit, and not in the letter; whose praise is not of men, but of God.
>
> Romans 2:28–29 (NKJ, italics mine)

> For I speak to you Gentiles; inasmuch as I am an apostle to the Gentiles, I magnify my ministry, if by any means I may provoke to jealousy those who are my flesh and save some of them. For if their being cast away is the reconciling of the world, what will their acceptance be but life from the dead? For if the first fruit is holy, the lump is also holy; and if the root is holy, so are the branches. And if some of the branches were broken off, and you, being a wild olive tree, were grafted in among them, and with them became a partaker of the root and fatness of the olive tree, do not boast against the branches. But if you do boast, remember that you do not support the root, but the root supports you. You will say then, "Branches were broken off that I might be grafted in." Well said. *Because of unbelief they were broken off, and you stand by faith. Do not be haughty, but fear. For if God did not spare the natural branches, He may not spare you either.* Therefore consider the goodness and severity of God: on those who fell, severity; but toward you, goodness, *if you continue in His goodness. Otherwise you also will be cut off. And they also, if they do not continue in unbelief, will be grafted in, for God is able to graft them in again.* For if you were cut out of the olive tree which is wild by nature, and were grafted contrary to nature into a cultivated olive tree, how much more will these, who are natural branches, be grafted into their own olive tree?
>
> Romans 11:13–24 (NKJV, italics mine)

From these we conclude that all Christians of every nationality join biological, converted Israel (Romans 11:25–29) to become a chosen generation, a royal priesthood, a holy nation, his own special people. What a blessing this is as you meditate on the significance and scope of Christ's royalty in God's kingdom.

**Jesus's Royal Subjects: The Kingdom of God**

But the purposes of God in Christ did not end with fulfilling the Davidic covenant and establishing Jesus as the King of kings and the Lord of lords. It remained for his Son to establish the nature and composition of his kingdom during his earthly visit. In fact, this became the principal purpose of all his teachings, as we noted earlier (Luke 4:43, 8:1).

The Sermon on the Mount (Matthew 5–7) and Matthew 13 are full of Christ's teachings on the priorities, values, and the spiritual nature of his kingdom. Among the most startling of these revelations is the one in which Jesus prioritizes the kingdom and God's righteousness above food and clothing!

> But seek first the kingdom of God and His righteousness, and all these things shall be added to you.
>
> MATTHEW 6:33 (NKJV)

In context, the "all these things" are basic necessities. Jesus's command here is that seeking and understanding the nature of God's kingdom and walking in God's righteousness are to be the first priorities of believers.

Interestingly, most Christians today are still waiting for the kingdom of God to come. Many expect the kingdom to come when Christ returns to earth at his second coming. Others expect it to exist only during the millennial age when Christ is personally king in Jerusalem. To the surprise of many, however, Jesus denies both of these interpretations in Luke 17. Note the following:

> Now when He was asked by the Pharisees when the kingdom of God would come, He answered them and said, "The kingdom of God does

> not come with observation; nor will they say, 'See here!' or 'See there!' For indeed, *the kingdom of God is within you.*"
>
> LUKE 17:20–21 (NKJV, ITALICS MINE)

The words translated "was asked" in this verse are actually derived from the verb *eperotao* (ἐπερωταώ[1]) in Greek, which is more accurately translated in the King James Version as "demanded." This verb is used when the one asking the question is talking to someone who is deemed inferior to himself, as in the case of a teacher to one of his students.[2] The question then carries the weight of a command.

The Pharisees were obviously frustrated trying to discover what Jesus was really doing. They heard his teachings, observed his miracles, and realized that they were dealing with a very powerful man. But politically speaking, it looked to them as if he had no power base upon which to establish any kingdom, let alone God's! He didn't consort among the rich and famous. He had no army. He had no political power or following. He didn't even have the confidence or the respect of the Jewish religious leaders! In fact, he frequently offended and challenged them by revealing their hypocrisy. (Note Matthew 23 for many such examples.) Finally, he was not publicly or privately plotting to get rid of the Romans or to set up Israel as the world's most powerful nation, things the Jewish establishment did expect of the Messiah.

Consequently, they were in no mood to beat around the bush about who he was and when he was going to establish the kingdom that he kept talking about. They demanded to know when he was going to make his move and set it up. Christ's answer was quite a surprise. The kingdom was to come without physical observation of any kind. Instead the kingdom of God was to dwell in the hearts and minds of believers. No one had anticipated this answer. It completely baffled the Pharisees.

Unfortunately, many Christians today also have not understood the implications of what Christ said. Note well that the physical return of Christ does not occur prior to his spiritual return to the hearts and minds of believers. We are to believe no one who says that "Jesus is now in India performing many wonderful miracles" or "I am the reincarnation of Christ" or "I am the last prophet of God." In Matthew 24 Jesus teaches and warns the following:

> Then if anyone says to you, "Look, here is the Christ!" or "There!" do not believe it. For false christs and false prophets will rise and show great signs and wonders to deceive, if possible, even the elect. See, I have told you beforehand. Therefore if they say to you, "Look, He is in the desert!" do not go out; or "Look, He is in the inner rooms!" do not believe it. For as the lightning comes from the east and flashes to the west, so also will the coming of the Son of Man be.
>
> MATTHEW 24:23–27 (NKJV)

Christ's description here clearly states that his second physical coming will be a very audiovisual event, like lightning from the east to the west. There will be a shout, and the sound of trumpets! (1 Thessalonians 4:16) This very loud and striking coming is clearly not what Jesus was talking about in the Luke 17 response to the Pharisees. Further, nothing written about the millennial kingdom accounts for its being within us. What is it then? How does this kingdom work?

The answer is simple and straightforward. When we have acted upon the gospel by confessing and repenting of our sins and inviting Jesus Christ into our life as our Lord and Savior, he comes! He abides in our hearts and our minds as the King and ruler of our lives. And when the King lives in our hearts and minds, then the kingdom of God resides within us. If you've never meditated about this or have never fully understood God's plan for salvation, meditate on the following verses:

> If we confess our sins, He is faithful and just to forgive us our sins and to cleanse us from all unrighteousness.
>
> 1 John 1:9 (NKJV)

*Confess* means to admit to God. We can't hide anything from God anyway, so we must have the humility and courage to admit our transgressions and allow Christ's grace and blood to cleanse us.

> Truly, these times of ignorance God overlooked, but now commands all men everywhere to repent.
>
> Acts 17:30 (NKJV)

*Repent* means "to turn around" or "change one's mind about." It means to change our attitude about our sins and turn away from them. The net result of true repentance is the cessation of the confessed sin in the person's life. John the Baptist, that great preacher of repentance and harbinger of Christ and his kingdom, put it this way:

> In those days John the Baptist came preaching in the wilderness of Judea, and saying, "Repent, for the kingdom of heaven is at hand!"... Then Jerusalem, all Judea, and all the region around the Jordan went out to him and were baptized by him in the Jordan, confessing their sins. But when he saw many of the Pharisees and Sadducees coming to his baptism, he said to them, "Brood of vipers! Who warned you to flee from the wrath to come? Therefore bear fruits worthy of repentance, and do not think to say to yourselves, 'We have Abraham as our father.' For I say to you that God is able to raise up children to Abraham from these stones. And even now the ax is laid to the root of the trees. Therefore every tree which does not bear good fruit is cut down and thrown into the fire."
>
> Matthew 3:1, 5–10 (NKJV)

Consequently, the sequence God is looking for is not "sin then confess, sin then confess," but "sin, confess, and repent." Our minds must change, and our attitudes toward our sins must change!

This genuine repentance must then be followed by an invitation to the King of kings and Lord of lords to enter our lives. When Jesus is invited in, he comes (Revelation 3:20; John 1:12–13); and when Christ comes in to rule, the kingdom of God and his righteous power is within (Luke 17:23 and John 14:12–14)!

In summary, then, the fourth major purpose for Christ's coming physically to the earth was to fulfill the prophetic promises that were made about him to establish his Davidic lineage, to fulfill the Abrahamic and Davidic covenants, and to teach and establish the foundations of the kingdom of God within each believer. All these things he did in full obedience to the Father with grace and truth.

## Establish the New Covenant

The fifth and last major purpose of God sending his Son Jesus the Christ was to establish a new covenant with the physical and spiritual descendants of Israel. This covenant was recorded in Zacharias's prophecy noted earlier, i.e., Luke 1:72–75; and it confirms that we will be granted deliverance from the hands of our enemies and serve God without fear, in holiness and righteousness all the days of our lives.

All of us who name the name of Jesus and fellowship together in a church or a group of believers have taken Holy Communion, celebrated the Lord's table, participated in the Lord's supper, celebrated Mass, or under some other name have received the body and blood of our Lord Jesus Christ as he commanded. Many of us have heard our pastor or priest repeat Christ's words of institution using a phrase similar to "this is the blood of the New Covenant which was shed for you and for many for the remission of sins, do this as often as you shall drink it in remembrance of Me." We've heard it so many times that most of us are no longer listening to it carefully. We miss the part about the new covenant, and we have little understanding about what it is or why it's significant. This is very unfortunate, since understanding the truth and power of Christianity without an understanding of the new covenant is impossible.

## Jeremiah's Prophecy

It is critical that we pause here to reflect on just what the new covenant is! To comprehend its implications, one must begin with the original declaration set down by the Prophet Jeremiah.

> "Behold, the days are coming, says the LORD, when I will make a new covenant with the house of Israel and with the house of Judah—not according to the covenant that I made with their fathers in the day that I took them by the hand to lead them out of the land of Egypt, My covenant which they broke, though I was a husband to them, says the LORD. But this is the covenant that I will make with the house of Israel after those days, says the LORD: I will put My law in their minds, and write it on their hearts; and I will be their God, and they shall be My people. No more shall every man teach his neighbor, and every man his brother, saying, 'Know the LORD,' for they all shall know Me, from the least of them to the greatest of them, says the LORD. For I will forgive their iniquity, and their sin I will remember no more."
>
> Jeremiah 31:31–34 (NKJV)

There is a lot to unpack here. First, note that this is the first time that a "new covenant" is mentioned in the Old Testament.

Until this point, Israel and Judah had been operating under the old covenant, which was essentially the law as revealed in the Pentateuch, the first five books of the Old Testament. In the book of Deuteronomy, Moses declares that this covenant is contained in the Ten Commandments and the attendant statutes and ordinances.

> So He declared to you His covenant which He commanded you to perform, the Ten Commandments; and He wrote them on two tablets of stone. And the LORD commanded me at that time to teach you statutes and judgments, that you might observe them in the land which you cross over to possess.
>
> DEUTERONOMY 4:13–14 (NKJV)

Further, God said to Israel through Moses that "if you will obey my commands and keep this covenant that I make with you, then I will bless you." In Deuteronomy 28:1–14, we see that God promises many beautiful blessings to Israel if they will only obey the terms of the covenant. Every form of prosperity—material, familial, meteorological, marital, spiritual, governmental, and positional—is promised. It is a truly wonderful passage of blessings:

> Now it shall come to pass, *if you diligently obey the voice of the LORD your God*, to observe carefully all His commandments which I command you today, that the LORD your God will set you high above all nations of the earth. "And all these blessings shall come upon you and overtake you, because you obey the voice of the LORD your God: 'Blessed shall you be in the city, and blessed shall you be in the country. Blessed shall be the fruit of your body, the produce of your ground and the increase of your herds, the increase of your cattle and the offspring of your flocks. Blessed shall be your basket and your kneading bowl. Blessed shall you be when you come in, and blessed shall you be when you go out. The LORD will cause your enemies who rise against you to be defeated before your face; they shall come out against you one way and flee before you seven ways. The LORD will command

> the blessing on you in your storehouses and in all to which you set your hand, and He will bless you in the land which the LORD your God is giving you. The LORD will establish you as a holy people to Himself, just as He has sworn to you, *if you keep the commandments of the LORD your God and walk in His ways.* Then all peoples of the earth shall see that you are called by the name of the LORD, and they shall be afraid of you. And the LORD will grant you plenty of goods, in the fruit of your body, in the increase of your livestock, and in the produce of your ground, in the land of which the LORD swore to your fathers to give you. The LORD will open to you His good treasure, the heavens, to give the rain to your land in its season, and to bless all the work of your hand. You shall lend to many nations, but you shall not borrow. And the LORD will make you the head and not the tail; you shall be above only, and not be beneath, *if you heed the commandments of the LORD your God, which I command you today, and are careful to observe them.* So you shall not turn aside from any of the words which I command you this day, to the right or the left, to go after other gods to serve them.'"
>
> Deuteronomy 28:1–14 (NKJV, italics mine)

God repeatedly interjects that these blessings are conditional on Israel's obeying his commandments. He warns Israel that if they do not keep the terms of their agreement (covenant), he will curse them. Deuteronomy 28:15–68 goes on to reveal fifty-four verses of curses that God himself will bring upon Israel if they break their promise to him. These include the opposites of all the blessings above plus diseases and even, in the event of total rejection and utter corruption, the dire promise that they would eat their own children (verses 53–58)! One need only recall the events surrounding the siege of Jerusalem (note Jeremiah 11:1–17 and 14:1–16) just before the Babylonian captivity and the siege of Masada and other places during the war with Rome about AD 70 to see that God quite literally keeps his every promise, even to the point of bringing the dreaded curses upon them when they break their promises to him.

Most Christians today do not think that God would ever curse people or repeat his destructive actions of history. And he won't, if we will obey his commands. He is our loving Father. But he will not spoil or destroy his children with empty threats, nor will he be unjust in his judgment. His love and mercy require his moving against sin and wickedness, which destroy harmony, peace, and righteousness in a people and a nation.

The Bible records that the Israelites were very optimistic when Moses read the covenant to them and asked for their ratification. They immediately accepted the covenant terms and conditions, thinking that they would only be blessed and that they would never turn away from God's commands.

> So Moses came and told the people all the words of the LORD and all the judgments. And all the people answered with one voice and said, *"All the words which the LORD has said we will do."* And Moses wrote all the words of the LORD. And he rose early in the morning, and built an altar at the foot of the mountain, and twelve pillars according to the twelve tribes of Israel. Then he sent young men of the children of Israel, who offered burnt offerings and sacrificed peace offerings of oxen to the LORD. And Moses took half the blood and put it in basins, and half the blood he sprinkled on the altar. Then he took the Book of the Covenant and read in the hearing of the people. *And they said, "All that the LORD has said we will do, and be obedient."* And Moses took the blood, sprinkled it on the people, and said, "This is the blood of the covenant which the LORD has made with you according to all these words."
>
> EXODUS 24:3–8 (NKJV, ITALICS MINE)

So Israel made a blood covenant with God that he would be their God and they would be his people. Further, they agreed to keep all of the laws and ordinances that God had commanded and be obedient.

Perusal of Joshua through Second Chronicles clearly reveals

that while often Israel wanted to obey, and sometimes did, for the most part they rebelled against his laws and committed spiritual adultery with the surrounding idols and religions. At the time that Jeremiah made his prophecy about the new covenant, Israel had already been divided and the ten tribes judged and cast off like chaff to the winds. Jerusalem itself was under attack by the Assyrians and was about to be taken into the Babylonian captivity. It was a bad time, and many of the curses promised in the first covenant were coming to pass, or had already come to pass, because of Israel's and Judah's rebellion against God.

## The Problem with the Old Covenant

It was at this time that God decided to make a new and different type of covenant with his chosen people. The first covenant was simply not working. The Jews had been rebellious ever since they crossed the Red Sea and entered the wilderness. And although they had good intentions, and many individuals did very well, for the most part they were unable or unwilling to follow God's laws. This resulted in much bloodshed, hatred, malice, and wickedness. Paul summarized this tragic state of ambivalence and failure in his Romans 7 description of how the *law of sin* triumphs over the *law of God* in the absence of the indwelling Holy Spirit.

> For I know that in me [that is, in my flesh] nothing good dwells; for to will is present with me, but how to perform what is good I do not find. For the good that I will to do, I do not do; but the evil I will not to do, that I practice. Now if I do what I will not to do, it is no longer I who do it, but *sin that dwells in me.* I find then a law, that evil is present with me, the one who wills to do good. For I delight in the *law of God* according to the inward man. But I see *another law* in my members, *warring* against the law of my mind, and bringing me into captivity

> to the *law of sin* which is in my members. O wretched man that I am! Who will deliver me from this body of death?
>
> ROMANS 7:18–24 (NKJV, ITALICS MINE)

There was nothing wrong with the old covenant per se as Paul so clearly affirms.

> For sin, taking occasion by the commandment, deceived me, and by it killed me. Therefore the law is holy, and the commandment holy and just and good.
>
> ROMANS 7:11–12 (NKJV)

Even Jesus upholds the law in his Sermon on the Mount.

> "*Do not think that I came to destroy the Law or the Prophets. I did not come to destroy but to fulfill.* For assuredly, I say to you, till heaven and earth pass away, one jot or one tittle will by no means pass from the law till all is fulfilled. Whoever therefore breaks one of the least of these commandments, and teaches men so, shall be called least in the kingdom of heaven; but whoever does and teaches them, he shall be called great in the kingdom of heaven. For I say to you, that unless your righteousness exceeds the righteousness of the scribes and Pharisees, you will by no means enter the kingdom of heaven."
>
> MATTHEW 5:17–20 (NKJV, ITALICS MINE)

The issue, therefore, was not the quality of the law or of the covenant. The concern was not even the teaching of the scribes and Pharisees (cf. Mat 23:2ff., 15:3–6). The problem was, first, the inability of the Jews to overcome the power of sin in their hearts and minds, and, second, the substitution of tradition, legalism, and hypocrisy for the righteousness of the law. Clinging to the letter and not the spirit of the law, they became religious, not righteous; hard, not merciful; cold, not loving; coy, not wise. And these issues were not overcome by the life and death of Jesus Christ. It remained for the Spirit of Christ (the Holy Spirit) to resolve these problems, and that will be covered in the next chapter.

## Communion as the Enduring Sign

The fifth and final purpose of Jesus, then, was to draw attention to the new covenant. This covenant enabled the law to be written on our hearts and in our minds, not just outside on tablets of stone, on a parchment, or in a book. And to ensure that his followers would never forget the means of implementing this new covenant, Jesus instituted the Last Supper. While eating together with his disciples, Jesus used two common elements of the Passover feast to symbolize his body and blood: the pierced unleavened bread and the last cup of wine. Since the modern church so frequently emphasizes just the forgiveness and remission of sins when offering communion, let's readjust our lenses and look at the total picture and the rich meanings of these two elements.

First, consider the spiritual meanings of the unleavened bread. From the scriptures that follow, one can see that it means Christ's body, eternal life, suffering, and sincerity and truth.

> For I received from the Lord that which I also delivered to you: that the Lord Jesus on the same night in which He was betrayed took bread; and when He had given thanks, He broke it and said, "Take, eat; this is My body which is broken for you; do this in remembrance of Me."
>
> 1 Corinthians 11:23–24 (NKJV)

> I am the living bread which came down from heaven. *If anyone eats of this bread, he will live forever*; and the bread that I shall give is My flesh, which I shall give for the life of the world.
>
> John 6:51 (NKJV, italics mine)

> Whoever eats My flesh and drinks My blood has eternal life, and I will raise him up at the last day.
>
> John 6:54 (NKJV)

> You shall eat no leavened bread with it; seven days you shall eat unleavened bread with it, that is, the bread of affliction (for you came out of the land of Egypt in haste), that you may remember the day in which you came out of the land of Egypt all the days of your life.
>
> Deuteronomy 16:3 (NKJV)

> Yes, and all who desire to live godly in Christ Jesus will suffer persecution.
>
> 2 Timothy 3:12 (NKJV)

> Therefore, let us keep the feast, not with old leaven, nor with the leaven of malice and wickedness, but with the unleavened bread of sincerity and truth.
>
> 1 Corinthians 5:8 (NKJV)

Now let's glean from the scriptures the rich and varied meanings of the wine. Cursory observation will reveal the following spiritual meanings: Christ's blood, his very life, his atonement, remission of sins, redemption, a clean conscience, and the new covenant. It is a powerful symbol indeed!

> For the life of the flesh is in the blood, and I have given it to you upon the altar to make atonement for your souls; for it is the blood that makes atonement for the soul.
>
> Leviticus 17:11 (NKJV)

> And according to the law almost all things are purified with blood, and without shedding of blood there is no remission.
>
> Hebrews 9:22 (NKJV)

> Not with the blood of goats and calves, but with His own blood He entered the Most Holy Place once for all, having obtained eternal redemption.
>
> HEBREWS 9:12 (NKJV)

> How much more shall the blood of Christ, who through the eternal Spirit offered Himself without spot to God, cleanse your conscience from dead works to serve the living God?
>
> HEBREWS 9:14 (NKJV)

> Then He took the cup, and gave thanks, and gave it to them, saying, "Drink from it, all of you. "For this is My blood of the new covenant, which is shed for many for the remission of sins."
>
> MATTHEW 26:27–28 (NKJV)

> Likewise He also took the cup after supper, saying, "This cup is the new covenant in My blood, which is shed for you."
>
> LUKE 22:20 (NKJV)

Churches around the world celebrate Communion, the Lord's table, or Holy Eucharist, at least once a month. Many celebrate it several times a week. From all the above, it should be clear to all of us why. It is the distillation of the gospel of Christ, and it is designed to remind us of the key elements of Christ's work on earth to save mankind. This celebration is to the modern church what the twelve stones from the Jordan were to the Jews crossing into the promised land (Joshua 4:20–24). It is the memorial of the blood covenant made between God and every believer who partakes spiritually of his Son's body and his blood, and a reminder that when our children ask us why we take Communion, we can answer them that it is to remind us of what God in Christ has done for us.

We will remember and remind them that Christ is in us and

we are in him (John 6:53), that we have his eternal life in us, that he has forgiven our sins and atoned for our souls, that affliction goes with a Christian's territory, and that sincerity and truth are the hallmarks of our walk. Further, we will remember that he has made a binding pact between himself and all of mankind, which gives all who will receive him whole new vistas and dimensions of understanding and blessing.

In summary, God's final purpose in Christ revealed in this remarkable prophecy of Zacharias in Luke was to establish the new covenant with Israel and, by extension, with all mankind. Then, having fulfilled all five major purposes through his life, death, and resurrection, and having returned after his resurrection to show himself alive by many infallible proofs (Acts 1:3), he gave the following commandment and then rose to the Father:

> And being assembled together with them, He commanded them not to depart from Jerusalem, but to wait for the Promise of the Father, "which," He said, "you have heard from Me; for John truly baptized with water, but you shall be baptized with the Holy Spirit not many days from now." Therefore, when they had come together, they asked Him, saying, "Lord, will You at this time restore the kingdom to Israel?" And He said to them, "It is not for you to know times or seasons which the Father has put in His own authority. But you shall receive power when the Holy Spirit has come upon you; and you shall be witnesses to Me in Jerusalem, and in all Judea and Samaria, and to the end of the earth."
>
> ACTS 1:4–8 (NKJV)

Through these words, Jesus proclaimed the next major step in God's plan for man's perfection: the baptism of the Holy Spirit. Jesus had visited, redeemed, saved, fulfilled, established, confirmed, and conquered. It was now the Holy Spirit's turn to fulfill his mighty purposes in God's wonderful plan for man's total renewal.

# The Purposes of God in the Holy Spirit

What Jesus was able to accomplish in three short years of ministry was nothing short of awesome! With wisdom, understanding, and obedience, he carried out the will of God in every aspect of his life. In so doing, he did everything necessary to save man and restore him to a personal relationship with God. But because he knew that man had a sinful nature, he realized it would take ongoing guidance and power to enable mankind to stay in relationship with God and to "serve Him without fear, in holiness and righteousness before Him, all the days of their life" (Luke 1:74–75). This is the overarching task of his Holy Spirit.

Therefore, after he spent forty days appearing to his disciples and encouraging them with infallible proofs that he had indeed overcome Satan, sin, and death and had established his kingdom on earth, he commanded them to remain in Jerusalem and wait for the promise of the Father. Why? Why did they have to stay in Jerusalem now? I'm sure that they felt excited and wanted to run right out and share Jesus with everyone. They had been very well trained, they had a lot of knowledge, they were eyewitnesses of Jesus' power and glory. They had lived with Jesus day in and day out for three years. If anyone knew him, if anyone had "doctorates" in Christianity, it was surely these eleven and the many others who had been with Jesus from the beginning. Why then did he restrain them from starting their ministries after he ascended?

To answer this question, we must return to the word of God and discover the other half of his plan for those whom Christ saved, which was to translate them into his kingdom by the empowerment of the Holy Spirit (Colossians 1:12–13; Ephesians 2:4–7). We must therefore consider the workings and the purposes of God in the Holy Spirit. It is to this end that this chapter is dedicated.

## Empower the Saints

First of all, Jesus knew that knowledge was not enough. The world was full of philosophers, teachers, religions, and disjointed knowledge of all kinds. But knowledge without wisdom is useless, and wisdom without understanding is vanity.

Let me attempt an illustration here. A professional football coach may know more than five hundred plays. That's knowledge. But if he is unable to put four plays together for his team to gain at least ten yards, then his knowledge is of little use. But if he is able to use his knowledge and the team's athletic gifts to move the ball and win the game, then he is deemed a wise coach. He was able to use specific knowledge at the appropriate times in order to attain a specific goal. But if he becomes puffed up and thinks that it was his play-calling wisdom that won the game, he becomes vain. Football is a team sport. One man, no matter how skilled or clever, cannot win a football game; it takes the whole team working together. Furthermore, it takes more than one game to win a season.

Consequently, if a coach is able to analyze both his own team's and the opponent teams' strengths and weaknesses and win most or all of the games he plays, humbly giving credit to the whole team, he is said to understand the game and be able to consistently apply his knowledge and use wisdom to maximize his team's gifts. "Wisdom is the principle thing; therefore get wisdom. And in all you're getting, get understanding" (Proverbs 4:7, NKJV).

So what's the point with regard to the disciples? Just this: Jesus knew that the disciples' knowledge and personal experience were not enough to enable them to victoriously share the gospel. Neither is it enough for a man or woman to attend a Bible college or seminary and say that they are now trained and able to share the gospel. If the disciples required more than that, how much more do we! Jesus knew that the disciples would be run over by Satan's ploys, frustrated with confusion, paralyzed with fear, puffed up with pride, sidetracked with administrative details, or wearied with busywork, plans, programs, or fund-raising. Peter, with great knowledge of Christ and of his kingdom, denied him three times and ran away, weeping when confronted with his own lack of courage (Matthew 26:69–75). The same will happen to any of us who think we can confront the world solely with knowledge and good preaching or teaching. We absolutely need God the Holy Spirit within us.

Note what happened to Peter after he received the Holy Spirit. He became as bold as a lion. He was not afraid to proclaim Christ publicly in the same place that he had denied him three times before (Acts 4:1–13). When in prison and facing death, he slept peacefully chained between two guards (Acts 12:1–7). Wow!

This same powerful transformation is precisely what is required for us today. The disciples needed to wait for the promise of the Father, and so do we. Jesus had explained to them that this promise was the baptism of the Holy Spirit. Then he said, "But you shall receive power when the Holy Spirit has come upon you; and you shall be witnesses to Me in Jerusalem, and in all Judea and Samaria, and to the end of the earth" (Acts 1:4–8, NKJV).

Notice that receiving the Holy Spirit's power precedes one's ability to be God's witnesses and to overcome all obstacles to effective and credible ministry. Why is that? The answer lies in the following amazing personal endowments of the Holy Spirit.

## New Birth

> Jesus answered and said to him, "Most assuredly, I say to you, unless one is born again, he cannot see the kingdom of God .... "Do not marvel that I said to you, 'You must be born again.' The wind blows where it wishes, and you hear the sound of it, but cannot tell where it comes from and where it goes. So is everyone who is born of the Spirit."
>
> JOHN 3:3, 7–8 (NKJV)

Beloved, Jesus says that we must be born again. *Born again* is not a denomination or another name for an evangelical Christian as many think. *Born again* is a phrasal verb that essentially means what it implies: we must have an entirely new outlook on life, a mental and spiritual rebirth. Our old, sinful nature is not acceptable. We need a brand-new heart and a brand-new way of looking at economics, politics, culture, morality, and life in general. We need a new worldview and an incorruptible and righteous standard. And we desperately need the ability and the will to lead a godly and righteous life.

As we shall see, all of these are contained in the gift of the Holy Spirit. And this gift is not restricted to some higher-power Christians. It is given to all believers who ask for it.

> If a son asks for bread from any father among you, will he give him a stone? Or if he asks for a fish, will he give him a serpent instead of a fish? Or if he asks for an egg, will he offer him a scorpion? If you then, being evil, know how to give good gifts to your children, how much more will your heavenly Father give the Holy Spirit to those who ask Him!
>
> LUKE 11:11–13 (NKJV)

On the other hand, the Holy Spirit is not an option for Christians either. It is not possible to be a victorious Christian without having the Holy Spirit in you.

> So then, those who are in the flesh cannot please God. But you are not in the flesh but in the Spirit, if indeed the Spirit of God dwells in you. Now *if anyone does not have the Spirit of Christ, he is not His.*
>
> Romans 8:8–9 (NKJV, italics mine)

Now this is a very strong statement, and it contains a lot of important information. If you do not have the Holy Spirit of Jesus Christ, you do not belong to him. It is simply not possible to say that one knows or belongs to Jesus without him. I think this will become more obvious as we consider more of the types of things that the Holy Spirit empowers a Christian to do and be.

Another vital literary and semantic issue disclosed in this verse is that the Spirit, the Spirit of God, and the Spirit of Christ are all used synonymously. This is all consistent with the doctrine of the Trinity, since indeed God the Father, God the Son, and God the Holy Spirit are one. They have different functions, and they have different purposes in the lives of each Christian, but they are one. Note the masculine singular Hebrew verb in Isaiah 48:16 and the unity disclosed in 1 John 5:7 below.

> Come ye near unto me, hear ye this; I have not spoken in secret from the beginning; from the time that it was, there am I: and now the Lord GOD, and his Spirit, hath sent me. [Note that the *hath* here is singular not plural and that the *I* is identified as "I am the first, I also am the last." As mentioned before, it is important to realize that "the Alpha and Omega, the First and the Last" is the description of Jesus Christ in Revelation 1:8–18.]
>
> Isaiah 48:16 (KJV)

> For there are three that bear record in heaven, the Father, the Word, and the Holy Ghost: and these three are one. [The *Word* here is also Jesus; cf. John 1:1, 14.]
>
> 1 JOHN 5:7 (KJV)

The *Shema* in Deuteronomy 6 also affirms this unity: "Hear, O Israel: The LORD our God, the LORD is one!" (Deuteronomy 6:4, NKJV) The fascinating and important observation here is that the word *God* in this verse is plural in the Hebrew, i.e., *Gods.*

A final distinction worthy of note in Romans 8:9 is Paul's contrasting "he who is in the flesh" with "he who is in the Spirit." Those who are in the flesh continue to do unrighteous acts, which prevent them from entering into the kingdom of God and make it impossible for them to please God. Examples of these works of the flesh are given by Paul in Galatians 5.

> For the flesh lusts against the Spirit, and the Spirit against the flesh; and these are contrary to one another, so that you do not do the things that you wish. But if you are led by the Spirit, you are not under the law. Now the works of the flesh are evident, which are: adultery, fornication, uncleanness, lewdness, idolatry, sorcery, hatred, contentions, jealousies, outbursts of wrath, selfish ambitions, dissensions, heresies, envy, murders, drunkenness, revelries, and the like; of which I tell you beforehand, just as I also told you in time past, that those who practice such things will not inherit the kingdom of God.
>
> GALATIANS 5:17–21(NKJV)

Therefore, for all these important reasons, we desperately need God's gracious provision of his Holy Spirit received through being born again. *Born again* is not just a title, but it is also the metaphorical representation of the total empowerment of our new life in Christ, which enables us to walk as he walked (1 John 2:6; Acts 1:8).

## New Heart

A corollary to the new birth above is the necessity for a new heart, a new center of feeling, character, and emotions. Since the natural man, the man who has not yet become a Christian, has a heart that Jeremiah by the Spirit describes as "desperately wicked," one can readily see that a person cannot simply give mental assent to biblical teachings and live as a Christian. He or she must have a brand-new heart, and this is precisely what God promises to each and every Christian who is in new covenant relationship with him.

> I will give you a new heart and put a new spirit within you; I will take the heart of stone out of your flesh and give you a heart of flesh. I will put My Spirit within you and cause you to walk in My statutes, and you will keep My judgments and do them.
>
> Ezekiel 36:26–27 (NKJV)

Note that God has promised in Ezekiel to give us a new heart. He's going to take away that heart of stone that through sin, discouragement, hatred, rejection, strife, or the like has become hard as a rock. And he's going to take that bitter, unloving, stubborn, proud, insensitive, unfeeling, harsh, broken heart and give us a new one. He is not going to try to fix our hearts or do bypass surgery. He's not going to put a bandage on our addictions or coddle our sins. He knows that our hearts are deceitful and desperately wicked (Jeremiah 17:9). No, he's going to give us a new heart: a heart of flesh. And flesh is warm and soft and alive. It is merciful, graceful, loving, kind, courteous, humble, caring, strong, and courageous. It is, in short, the heart of Christ. It is the only heart that can weather and overcome the vicissitudes of life with equanimity, steadfastness, and joy.

> But this is the covenant that I will make with the house of Israel after those days, says the LORD: I will put My law in their minds, and write it on their hearts; and I will be their God, and they shall be My people.
>
> JEREMIAH 31:33 (NKJV)

God is also going to do something to our new heart that is entirely unique, according to Jeremiah. He's going to write his laws on our hearts and in our minds. No longer will his statutes just be in the Bible or some theology book on the shelves of our libraries, which, when they are out of sight, are out of mind. No, they'll be ever-present engravings, available as worldview and behavioral filters, consciously and unconsciously, at all times. What a brilliant plan! The implications for Christian perfection here are enormous.

And what magnificent joy we have knowing that out of this new heart flows abundantly all the fruits of the Holy Spirit, which formed it. While Christians do not receive all the gifts of the Spirit, they do receive all of the fruits! These fruits are a package deal. They are the natural fruit of the Vine, Jesus Christ, within us (John 15:1–7). What are these fruits? Galatians 5:22–23 tells us the following:

> But the fruit of the Spirit is love, joy, peace, longsuffering, kindness, goodness, faithfulness, gentleness, self-control. Against such there is no law. And those who are Christ's have crucified the flesh with its passions and desires. If we live in the Spirit, let us also walk in the Spirit.
>
> GALATIANS 5:22–25 (NKJV)

Note that there is no law against any of these things in any nation. In fact, every people group on earth, and even creation itself, is awaiting the manifestation of these fruits in God's people:

> For the earnest expectation of the creation eagerly waits for the revealing of the sons of God. For the creation was subjected to futility, not willingly, but because of Him who subjected it in hope; because the creation itself also will be delivered from the bondage of corruption into the glorious liberty of the children of God
>
> Romans 8:19–21 (NKJV)

The concept of a new heart is by no means exhausted by this short précis. It has a much wider scope and range of application. Nevertheless, for purposes of our investigation of the enablers of Christian perfection, suffice it to say that having the heart of the Holy Spirit is a vitally important empowerment for the believer, which facilitates the proper attitudes and emotions required for godly living. Just the fruit of love alone covers all sins and removes bitterness, unforgiveness, hatred, strife, envy, murder, vengeance, mockery, crude jokes, and the like. A heart so filled and motivated by God's love is a powerhouse for righteousness and bondage-breaking.

## New Parent

Another amazing corollary to the concept of being born again and being baptized by and filled with the Holy Spirit is that of having a brand-new Father. When we invite Jesus Christ and his Holy Spirit into our lives, he comes! And when he does, God adopts us as his very own children. Look what the Word of God says about this transaction:

> But as many as received Him, to them He gave the right to become children of God, to those who believe in His name: who were born, not of blood, nor of the will of the flesh, nor of the will of man, but of God.
>
> John 1:12–13 (NKJV)

> For as many as are led by the Spirit of God, these are sons of God. For you did not receive the spirit of bondage again to fear, but you received the Spirit of adoption by whom we cry out, "Abba, Father." The Spirit Himself bears witness with our spirit that we are children of God, and if children, then heirs—heirs of God and joint heirs with Christ, if indeed we suffer with Him, that we may also be glorified together.
>
> ROMANS 8:14–17 (NKJV)

By the Holy Spirit we received adoption into the family of God. Note that we are not the natural children of God. Jesus Christ is the only begotten Son of God. We do not become other "Christs" as some cults have erroneously begun to assert. Although Jesus is now spiritually our stepbrother, he is, and will always be, our one and only Lord and Savior. Being an adopted child of God does not change this positional relationship. It does, however, grant us many new privileges, including the right to call God the Father "Daddy" (Abba) and to have a joint inheritance in the kingdom of God with Jesus. Praise God that he not only saved us, but that he also adopted us as his own children!

This is no small blessing. The hope of eternal life with God in heaven as one of his beloved children is one of the anchors of every Christian's soul (Hebrew 6:18–19). Jesus said the following:

> Let not your heart be troubled; you believe in God, believe also in Me. In My Father's house are many mansions; if it were not so, I would have told you. I go to prepare a place for you. And if I go and prepare a place for you, I will come again and receive you to Myself; that where I am, there you may be also.
>
> JOHN 14:1–3 (NKJV)

John also records this beautiful promise for God's adopted children:

> And this is the testimony: that God has given us eternal life, and this life is in His Son. He who has the Son has life; he who does not have the Son of God does not have life. These things I have written to you who believe in the name of the Son of God, that you may know that you have eternal life, and that you may continue to believe in the name of the Son of God.
>
> 1 John 5:11–13 (NKJV)

What a wonderful blessing adoption by God is. While many of us have had wonderful earthly fathers, the fact is that many others have not. Few have had godly fathers, and none has had a perfect one. Now, through the Holy Spirit, all born-again believers have a new and perfect Father: God. And he will be with us forever!

## New Citizenship

Furthermore, with this new paternity in Christ comes a new nationality. We're no longer citizens of Europe or America or Asia or Africa or any specific nation within these or other global regions. We have been translated into the kingdom of God by the new birth and are now citizens of heaven. We're only pilgrims here on earth awaiting our final resurrection into heaven.

> For our citizenship is in heaven, from which we also eagerly wait for the Savior, the Lord Jesus Christ, who will transform our lowly body that it may be conformed to His glorious body, according to the working by which He is able even to subdue all things to Himself.
>
> Philippians 3:20–21 (NKJV)

> Giving thanks to the Father who has qualified us to be partakers of the inheritance of the saints in the light. He has delivered us from the power of darkness and conveyed [KJV-translated] us into the kingdom of the Son of His love.
>
> Colossians 1:12–13 (NKJV)

> But you are a chosen generation, a royal priesthood, a holy nation, His own special people, that you may proclaim the praises of Him who called you out of darkness into His marvelous light; who once were not a people but are now the people of God, who had not obtained mercy but now have obtained mercy. Beloved, I beg you as sojourners and pilgrims, abstain from fleshly lusts which war against the soul.
>
> 1 PETER 2:9–11 (NKJV)

The Bible says that we have had a spiritual resurrection. We've gone from a life of sin and wickedness on earth directly, without seeing death, to a life of victory in the heavenly places. Consider carefully the following two verses:

> But God, who is rich in mercy, because of His great love with which He loved us, even when we were dead in trespasses, made us alive together with Christ (by grace you have been saved), and raised us up together, and made us sit together in the heavenly places *in Christ Jesus.*
>
> EPHESIANS 2:4–6 (NKJV, ITALICS MINE)

> If then you were raised with Christ, seek those things which are above, where Christ is, sitting at the right hand of God. Set your mind on things above, not on things on the earth. For you died, and *your life is hidden with Christ in God.*
>
> COLOSSIANS 3:1 (NKJV, ITALICS MINE)

Beloved, we are now the citizens of the kingdom of heaven, and we are subject to the laws and will of God. And while the Bible says clearly that we must honor those who rule over us on earth and that we must obey the laws of the land in which we live, it also affirms that in any case where the laws of the land conflict with the laws of God, we must obey the laws of God. Why? Because the kingdom of God is the country of our citizenship. We are sojourners in a foreign land wherever we live on earth.

Let every soul be subject to the governing authorities. For there is no authority except from God, and the authorities that exist are appointed by God. Therefore whoever resists the authority resists the ordinance of God, and those who resist will bring judgment on themselves. For rulers are not a terror to good works, but to evil. Do you want to be unafraid of the authority? Do what is good, and you will have praise from the same. For he is God's minister to you for good. But if you do evil, be afraid; for he does not bear the sword in vain; for he is God's minister, an avenger to execute wrath on him who practices evil. Therefore you must be subject, not only because of wrath but also for conscience' sake. For because of this you also pay taxes, for they are God's ministers attending continually to this very thing. Render therefore to all their due: taxes to whom taxes are due, customs to whom customs, fear to whom fear, honor to whom honor.

Romans 13:1–7 (NKJV)

Therefore submit yourselves to every ordinance of man for the Lord's sake, whether to the king as supreme, or to governors, as to those who are sent by him for the punishment of evildoers and for the praise of those who do good. For this is the will of God, that by doing good you may put to silence the ignorance of foolish men— as free, yet not using liberty as a cloak for vice, but as bondservants of God. Honor all people. Love the brotherhood. Fear God. Honor the king.

1 Peter 2:13–17 (NKJV)

And they (the Sanhedrin, the rulers, Scribes, the High Priest, and elders of Israel) called them and commanded them not to speak at all nor teach in the name of Jesus. But Peter and John answered and said to them, "Whether it is right in the sight of God to listen to you more than to God, you judge."

Acts 4:18–19 (NKJV)

> But Peter and the other apostles answered and said: "We ought to obey God rather than men."
>
> ACTS 5:29 (NKJV)

From all the above it is clear that if there are conflicting laws between God and man, we must obey God. But it is also imperative that we be careful not to simply say, "God or the Holy Spirit told me ...." The Word clearly says we need to test the spirits to see if they are from the Lord (1 John 4:1). Therefore, any time someone tells us that God said to disobey a law of man or do anything that contradicts specific scriptural directives, or the spirit of these directives, we must refrain from heeding or following that person and instead adhere to the scriptures. The reason for this is clearly stated in the following:

> All Scripture is given by inspiration of God, and is profitable for doctrine, for reproof, for correction, for instruction in righteousness, that the man of God may be complete [KJV-perfect], thoroughly equipped for every good work.
>
> 2 TIMOTHY 3:16–17 (NKJV)

> Knowing this first, that no prophecy of Scripture is of any private interpretation, for prophecy never came by the will of man, but holy men of God spoke as they were moved by the Holy Spirit.
>
> 2 PETER 1:20–21 (NKJV)

> Jesus Christ is the same yesterday, today, and forever.
>
> HEBREWS 13:8 (NKJV)

God is unchanging, and the laws of his kingdom are unchanging. Jesus himself said that he did not come to destroy the law, or the prophets, but to fulfill them (Matthew 5:17–18). And that is precisely what he did with his teaching, his character, and his life.

Therefore, it is easy for Christians who have been empowered by the Spirit to know the laws of this kingdom. They are written in the Bible, confirmed by the Holy Spirit (Ezekiel 36:27), and written on our hearts by God (Jeremiah 31:33). Therefore there need be no ambiguity about the content, the spirit, or the intent of these laws.

Now perhaps, beloved, you will understand why Jesus said, "But seek ye first the kingdom of God, and his righteousness, and all these things will be added unto you" (Matthew 6:33 KJV). When we understand kingdom principles and have obtained the keys thereof through the Holy Spirit, then we see clearly why seeking his kingdom, understanding his righteousness, and being empowered to walk in his righteousness unlock the blessings of his love.

## New Mind

Consider for a moment one of Paul's most shocking announcements: "But we have the mind of Christ" (1 Corinthians 2:16). Try meditating on this statement this coming week. The simplicity of the declaration is disarming, but its multifaceted implications for our actions are astounding. Is this an isolated verse? Is this out of context? Consider the additional support for this verse:

> But the *natural man does not receive the things of the Spirit of God*, for they are foolishness to him; nor can he know them, because they are spiritually discerned. But he who is spiritual judges all things, yet he himself is rightly judged by no one. For "who has known the mind of the LORD that he may instruct Him?" But *we have the mind of Christ.*
>
> 1 Corinthians 2:14–16 (NKJV, italics mine)

> Fulfill my joy by being like-minded, having the same love, being of one accord, of one mind. Let nothing be done through selfish ambition or conceit, but in lowliness of mind let each esteem others better than himself. Let each of you look out not only for his own interests,

> but also for the interests of others. *Let this mind be in you which was also in Christ Jesus.*
>
> PHILIPPIANS 2:2–5 (NKJV, ITALICS MINE)

> Now I plead with you, brethren, by the name of our Lord Jesus Christ, that you all speak the same thing, and that there be no divisions among you, but that you be perfectly joined together in the same mind and in the same judgment.
>
> 1 CORINTHIANS 1:10 (NKJV)

> I implore Euodia and I implore Syntyche to be of the same mind in the Lord.
>
> PHILIPPIANS 4:2 (NKJV)

> Only let your conduct be worthy of the gospel of Christ, so that whether I come and see you or am absent, I may hear of your affairs, that you stand fast in one spirit, *with one mind* striving together for the faith of the gospel.
>
> PHILIPPIANS 1:27 (NKJV, ITALICS MINE)

> Therefore, since Christ suffered for us in the flesh, arm yourselves also with the *same mind*, for he who has suffered in the flesh has ceased from sin.
>
> 1 PETER 4:1 (NKJV, ITALICS MINE)

There are many more verses in the Scriptures having to do with being like-minded. Some deal with specific issues of agreement and others the more universal mind of Christ. The first one mentioned above, however, is the most general and the most important for the issue at hand. It makes the most crucial observation of all, that the natural man, the one who is not a Christian and has neither received Jesus Christ as his Lord and Savior nor invited the Holy Spirit into his life, does not receive the things of the Spirit of God. He or she simply is not equipped to know, understand, or even desire the things of the Spirit, for they are foolishness to him. He will accept neither the clear admonitions of the Scriptures nor the promptings of the Holy Spirit; for, although he may understand them, he is not willing to submit to their truths.

Genuine Christians, however, are different. They have been born again as defined above, and they have received the mind of Christ. This has many implications for their way of thinking and acting. The following is a short list:

**Loving Enemies Becomes Reasonable**

Jesus' command "Love your enemies, bless them that curse you, do good to them that hate you, and pray for them who despitefully use you, and persecute you" (Matthew 5:44, KJV) now seems reasonable and doable. Before, believers would just laugh this command off and say, "That's impossible!" But now, with the heart and mind of Christ, they are empowered to behave as he did. He forgave those who killed him. He offered them salvation, he wept for them, he fed and healed many, and he and his disciples shared the gospel with them. He never took revenge on his persecutors, and he even rebuked Peter for trying to do so. True believers can do the same (John 18:10–11; Matthew 26:51–53).

**Obedience Becomes Natural**

We will *want* to keep God's commandments, and we will be able to do so. Since God has written his commandments on our hearts and *on our minds* (Jeremiah 31:34), they will not be burdensome to us. On the contrary, they will be our delight. When we obey them naturally out of love, they will be evidence that we know Jesus.

> By this we know that we love the children of God, when we love God and keep His commandments. For this is the love of God, that we keep His commandments. And His commandments are not burdensome.
>
> 1 JOHN 5:2–3 (NKJV)

> And hereby we do know that we know him, if we keep his commandments. He who says, "I know Him," and does not keep His commandments, is a liar, and the truth is not in him. But whoever keeps His word, truly the love of God is perfected in him. By this we know that we are in Him.
>
> 1 JOHN 2:3–5 (KJV)

## Humility Replaces Pride

> Let nothing be done through selfish ambition or conceit, but in lowliness of mind let each esteem others better than himself.
>
> PHILIPPIANS 2:3 (NKJV)

Humility should not be hard for Christians with the mind of Christ and the knowledge that all men are created in the image of God. Everyone is unique in some way. I've never met a person who couldn't do something better than I could. Frequently I have been amazed at what many people would consider even "common" skills. While on a predawn prayer walk in Baguio City, the Philippines, one morning, I chanced upon a street sweeper. I was amazed at how she had taken a piece of bamboo and arranged several stiff coconut leaf midribs, *walis tingting* in Filipino, in a cone shape around one end. It made a very light and efficient broom, but I could not figure out how she'd made it. So I stopped her and asked if I could see how she had done it. She happily obliged, and I treated myself to a simple and ingenious method of fastening the ribs around a ball at the end of a bamboo stick. I really appreciated this woman for her artistry and her work for the community.

Humility is often a problem, however, when we lead groups

or represent or head governments or organizations. Nevertheless, God's standards remain the same: he hates pride and the lust for power and glory. Consider the scriptural admonitions on these issues:

> But He gives more grace. Therefore He says: "God resists the proud, But gives grace to the humble."
>
> James 4:6 (NKJV)

> Pride goes before destruction, And a haughty spirit before a fall.
>
> Proverbs 16:18 (NKJV)

> Do not lift up your horn on high; Do not speak with a stiff neck. For exaltation comes neither from the east Nor from the west nor from the south. But God is the Judge: He puts down one, And exalts another.
>
> Psalm 75:5–7 (NKJV)

> These six things the LORD hates, Yes, seven are an abomination to Him: A proud look, A lying tongue, Hands that shed innocent blood, A heart that devises wicked plans, Feet that are swift in running to evil, A false witness who speaks lies, And one who sows discord among brethren.
>
> Proverbs 6:16 (NKJV)

> I am the LORD, that is My name; And My glory I will not give to another, Nor My praise to carved images.
>
> Isaiah 42:8 (NKJV)

> Thus says the LORD: "Let not the wise man glory in his wisdom, Let not the mighty man glory in his might, Nor let the rich man glory in his riches; But let him who glories glory in this, That he understands and knows Me, That I am the LORD, exercising loving kindness,

> judgment, and righteousness in the earth. For in these I delight," says the LORD.
>
> JEREMIAH 9:23–24 (NKJV)

In the Philippines, many memoranda between government officials are signed with the salutation "more power." Presumably they intend the statement as a compliment to their peer or their boss. What they forgot are the last words of the Lord's Prayer: "for *thine* is the kingdom and *the power and the glory* forever and ever, amen" (italics mine). God will not share his kingdom, his power, or his glory with another (Isaiah 42:8).

Lord Acton once said, "Power tends to corrupt, and absolute power corrupts absolutely. Great men are almost always bad men."[1] While perhaps a bit overstated, the previous century has had more than its share of power and glory seekers who have demonstrated Acton's point. Many individuals have killed or injured millions in their thirst for both. Stalin, Hitler, Hirohito, Idi Amin, Khomeini, Saloth Sar Pol Pot, Saddam Hussein, and Osama Bin Laden are but a few of this ignoble class. But they are only the most well known. Unfortunately, our sinful nature prompts all of us to self-centeredness and a desire for power and glory. That is why it is so important to have the mind of Christ to overcome this scourge of human nature.

Consider how God showed his humility by sending his only begotten Son as a baby, born in a manger to powerless newlyweds of a rural village in Israel, and then employing him as a carpenter with no political, military, or religious power contacts at all. Our King of kings and Lord of lords came as an itinerant missionary with no permanent address and no place to lay his head! He was the most powerful man ever to walk on the earth, yet he never used his power for his own aggrandizement. Not even to save his own life. Not even to anesthetize the pain. Not even to get even for his mistreatment or to prove that he was right and they were wrong.

Would we do the same? What if we had the mind of Christ? We do. Think about it.

At this point, an important caveat to having the mind of Christ must be mentioned. There are passages in the Scriptures that either directly state, or indirectly intimate, that we do not have the thoughts of God and that we do not have his mind. And it is absolutely true that we do not have the totality of the mind of Christ as the resurrected Son of God. We do not have the omniscience of God. We do not have all his thoughts. We do not know what all his plans are for individuals or even for most of the events of history. We do not know all his tactics or strategies. In short, having the mind of Christ does not make us demigods. Consider the following:

> Let the wicked forsake his way, And the unrighteous man his thoughts; Let him return to the LORD, And He will have mercy on him; And to our God, For He will abundantly pardon. "For My thoughts are not your thoughts, Nor are your ways My ways," says the LORD. "For as the heavens are higher than the earth, So are My ways higher than your ways, And My thoughts than your thoughts. For as the rain comes down, and the snow from heaven, And do not return there, But water the earth, And make it bring forth and bud, That it may give seed to the sower And bread to the eater, So shall My word be that goes forth from My mouth; It shall not return to Me void, But it shall accomplish what I please, And it shall prosper in the thing for which I sent it."
>
> Isaiah 55:7–11 (NKJV)

> Oh, the depth of the riches both of the wisdom and knowledge of God! How unsearchable are His judgments and His ways past finding out! "For who has known the mind of the LORD? Or who has become His counselor?"
>
> Romans 11:33–34 (NKJV)

The same author, who, by the Spirit, said that we have the mind of Christ, implies, by the same Spirit, that we cannot know the mind of the Lord. But there are no conflicts in the Scriptures. God does not contradict himself. What he is saying is that receiving the Holy Spirit empowers us, as children of God still in the flesh, to live a just and righteous life and to have all that is necessary of the mind of Christ to do that. In short, we do have the mind of Christ, just not all of it. But we do have enough of it: enough to totally carry out the plans that God has for each of our lives, enough to transform us by the renewing of our minds, enough to bring us to the life of a perfect man, and enough to conform us to the image of his Son (Romans 12:2; Ephesians 4:13; Romans 8:29–30). Notice especially Isaiah 55:11 above: "My word ... shall prosper in the thing to which I sent it." Jesus is the word of God, and he is in us (John 1:1, 14; Romans 8:9–10; Colossians 1:25–29)! Therefore, we, as Christ-filled Christians, shall be prospered.

**His Works Become Our Works**

When we have the mind of Christ, we will do the same things that he did, and we will do them joyfully and in singleness of heart. We will also be delighted in the gifts that God has given to others and will esteem others better than ourselves.

> Most assuredly, I say to you, he who believes in Me, the works that I do he will do also; and greater works than these he will do, because I go to My Father.
>
> JOHN 14:12 (NKJV)

Therefore, beloved, it should come as no surprise when we hear of miraculous healings, demons being cast out, or even people being raised from the dead. These are the promised results of the mind and heart of God working in his servants. And nowhere in the Bible does it say that these gifts will cease after the twelve apostles. Many current missionaries and evangelists are eyewitnesses to one or more of these things and don't think them strange or out-of-the-ordinary Christian experiences.

Jackie and I, for example, have witnessed the Lord cast out many demons and heal many people. One of our acquaintances, a student from Bangladesh at the Asia Pacific Theological Seminary (Assemblies of God), related to us his eyewitness experience of a man being raised from the dead by the Lord. These events always increase the faith of believers and frequently lead to many conversions as people seek to know the Lord who has this kind of power and love.

But not all miracles yield positive results. Some bring conflict with unbelievers or with "believers" who refuse to acknowledge God's power and willingness to do miracles in the modern day. Let me share just one personal illustration.

About two years after we arrived in the Philippines, my senior pastor's wife called me at midnight and asked me to please come quickly to the *barangay* captain's (village leader's) home next door to the church. I knew her husband was out of town, so I asked what the problem was. She said that the captain had called to ask for help for his son. He had gone "wild" in his home and had supernatural strength. He had been subdued by many men, but his eyes were still "wild." I told her I would be right over. When I arrived, the son, whom I estimated to be around twenty-one years old, was lying quietly on the bed. There were six men in the room to grab him if he tried to run. They had a Bible at his head, a rosary around his neck, and salt at his feet (an animist "protection" to ward off the evil spirits). They said that they had been praying for him for about six hours, but nothing had changed since he was "afflicted." I sat down on a chair facing his bed and began to pray. The young man rose from his supine position and sat cross-legged on top of the bed directly across from me, looking me in the eyes. His eyes were unblinking, penetrating, and fixed. I could tell that he was sizing me up. I kept praying. I did not have much experience with this type of ministry, and I was very aware of the seven sons of Sceva in Acts 19. I really prayed for the Lord to protect me and to give me the wisdom I needed about what to say and to do. I don't remember exactly what I was praying at that time, but I do recall that the blood of Jesus came to my mind. Slowly, I saw the young man's body tense up, but neither his snakelike eyes nor his body moved. I knew something was going to happen. I kept praying. Suddenly, he sprang off the bed and bolted for the door. The six men caught him and threw him back on the bed. He went back to the lotus position, tense and staring at my eyes. I then prayed in earnest the blood of Jesus and commanded the spirit to leave in the name of Jesus of Nazareth. His body went limp and his contorted face relaxed and looked normal. He went immediately to his knees and thanked the Lord for releasing him.

The battle had been won, but the war was not over. For two weeks he faithfully attended Bible studies in which I shared the gospel more fully to him. Unfortunately, his family was Catholic/animist and his sister, who also lived in the compound and at whose home we held the studies, was a Mormon. Whether the influence of family, syncretistic beliefs, cults, sin, my inability to communicate effectively, or some other spiritual entity weakened his faith, I do not know. But over time he became less faithful in attendance and finally stopped altogether. I haven't seen him since.

Obviously, I had mixed emotions as a result of this experience. On the one hand, I was very glad that he hadn't attacked me and that the Lord had cast out the demon. I knew it was a miracle and a personal blessing (Mark 9:38–39; Luke 10:17–20). But I had hoped to see the young man blossom into a strong believer who could have witnessed to his family and friends for the Lord. Perhaps others had that joy later as they watered and God granted the increase (1 Corinthians 3:6–8). Or perhaps the Lord was using this experience to show me the importance of the parable of the sower (Matthew 13:3–23) and to teach me not to rely on signs and wonders to bring people to a saving faith in Christ (John 2:23–25, 12:37). Only a personal, born-again, loving relationship with Jesus Christ saves people, and that is only possible if the Father draws that person to him (John 6:44).

The major point here, however, is that God is continuing to use his people to share the gospel with all mankind, and he is confirming their faithful word with signs and wonders following as the scripture promises (Mark 16:20). He is doing so in the same way and for the same reason as expressed by Paul: "And my speech and my preaching was not with enticing words of man's wisdom, but in demonstration of the Spirit and of power: That your faith should not stand in the wisdom of men, but in the power of God" (1 Corinthians 2:4, KJV).

An important corollary to the demonstration of God's power, however, is the humble attitude with which the saint utilizes his or her gifts. As mentioned, God shares his glory with no man, and he hates pride (Isaiah 42:8, Proverbs 8:13). One of the greatest dangers of being used by God in a powerful way is pride of accomplishment: the feeling that somehow God loves us more than other saints by giving us a gift of healing or miracles, and then using the gift as if the result and power were ours and not an extension of God's purposes and power for the life of the recipient. As a corrective to this temptation, the scriptures admonish us to esteem others better than ourselves, and they remind us that the poor in spirit obtain the kingdom of heaven and the meek inherit the earth (Matthew 5:3, 6).

**Unity Stems from Christ Within**

One of the buzzwords in Christendom today is *unity* or ecumenism. In recent years, there have been several efforts to arrange interdenominational meetings with the intent of establishing a dialogue between denominations that would result in a reunification of the church. Sadly, because of the diverse theological and doctrinal differences, little ground has been gained beyond the willingness to cooperate and "overlook" differences for the sake of the gospel. While this has had salubrious affects in many parts of the world, it has nonetheless overlooked the biblical essential, which establishes the basis of true unity: the mind of Christ. The church is the body of Christ composed of born-again members with the mind of Christ. Consider the following:

> I now rejoice in my sufferings for you, and fill up in my flesh what is lacking in the afflictions of Christ, for the sake of His body, which is the church.
>
> COLOSSIANS 1:24 (NKJV)

> You also, as living stones, are being built up a spiritual house, a holy priesthood, to offer up spiritual sacrifices acceptable to God through Jesus Christ.
>
> 1 PETER 2:5 (NKJV)

> And He put all things under His feet, and gave Him to be head over all things to the church, which is His body, the fullness of Him who fills all in all.
>
> EPHESIANS 1:22–23 (NKJV)

Several places in Scripture make this last point: the church is the body of Jesus Christ. Jesus did not come to earth to set up multiple churches or denominations with multiple theologies. No, he came to establish his kingdom and his church. So here's the point: the mind of Christ, like his Holy Spirit, is not fragmented or schizophrenic. Jesus is the truth, and his Spirit is the Spirit of truth. How then can pastors, teachers, theologians, bishops, etc.—all of whom claim to have the mind of Christ, the Holy Spirit, and the truth—hold conflicting views on Christian ethics and doctrines?

While there were disputes in the book of Acts over circumcision, ceremonial and dietary laws, and other Jewish issues, there appears to be little or no conflict among New Testament writers concerning basic doctrines of the faith. Therefore, the proliferation of Christian denominations and "Christian" cults that we see today has weakened the church and called into question the very essence of the body that Christ established.

Unity in the church cannot be established by ecumenical movements in Catholicism or evangelicalism. It is not an issue of pacification, conformity, submission, blending, cooperating, yielding, or influence-peddling. It is not a political or management objective. It is not a sharing of power or democratic process. It is not an economic issue. Succinctly, it is having and expressing the mind of Christ. Furthermore, the whole purpose of the Holy Spirit's ministerial gifts is to bring the church to the unity of faith and to the fullness of Jesus Christ.

> And He Himself gave some to be apostles, some prophets, some evangelists, and some pastors and teachers, for the equipping of the saints for the work of ministry, for the edifying of the body of Christ, till we all come to the *unity of the faith* and of the knowledge of the Son of God, to a perfect man, to the *measure of the stature of the fullness of Christ.*
>
> Ephesians 4:11–13 (NKJV, italics mine)

Notice that God has given his apostles, prophets, evangelists, pastors, and teachers "until we all come to the unity of the faith," until we've become "perfect men," and until all of our church members attain "the stature of the fullness of Christ." Are these the stated goals of our churches today? Are these the foci of our seminaries, Bible colleges, discipleship programs and Bible studies? Are we willing to abandon the carnal church of 1 Corinthians 3:3–4 and pick up the higher vision of the living church of Ephesians 4:13?

True unity in the church is only possible through having the same mind and heart: that of Jesus Christ. As we abide in him and he abides in us, that mind and heart grows in us. As we understand more and more of his actions and motives through the Holy Spirit within us, our worldview blends with and submits to his. Furthermore, the reality of a harmonious, organic unity in him ala 1 Corinthians 12:4–27 and Romans 12:4–5 becomes the joyful and credible goal of the church. This is the practical result of the "mystery" that was hidden from the Gentiles, which Paul talks about in Colossians 1:26–27.

Therefore, the only genuine hope for unity and perfection in the church is having the mind of Christ. God has given us this hope and assurance through his Spirit. While Christian unity is both possible and attainable in Christ Jesus, it is not possible as a work in the flesh with all "churches" or religions. In fact, attempts to "unify" without the mind of Christ can be dangerous for the flock. Consider carefully the warnings of Paul:

> Do not be unequally yoked together with unbelievers. For what fellowship has righteousness with lawlessness? And what communion has light with darkness? And what accord has Christ with Belial? Or what part has a believer with an unbeliever? And what agreement has the temple of God with idols? For you are the temple of the living God. As God has said: "I will dwell in them And walk among them. I will be their God, And they shall be My people." Therefore "Come out from among them And be separate, says the Lord. Do not touch what is unclean, And I will receive you."
>
> 2 CORINTHIANS 6:14–17 (NKJV)

> Now the Spirit expressly says that in latter times some will depart from the faith, giving heed to deceiving spirits and doctrines of demons, speaking lies in hypocrisy, having their own conscience seared with a hot iron.
>
> 1 TIMOTHY 4:1 (NKJV)

> I charge you therefore before God and the Lord Jesus Christ, who will judge the living and the dead at His appearing and His kingdom: Preach the word! Be ready in season and out of season. Convince, rebuke, exhort, with all longsuffering and teaching. For the time will come when they will not endure sound doctrine, but according to their own desires, because they have itching ears, they will heap up for themselves teachers; and they will turn their ears away from the truth, and be turned aside to fables.
>
> 2 Timothy 4:1–4 (NKJV)

## New Strength

It is hard to give adequate superlatives when talking about the Holy Spirit. Every empowerment given to man is awesome in its own right. But probably the most underrated of all the empowerments that God gave us through his Spirit was the power to overcome sin in our lives. When I first realized what God had done in this area, I was dumbfounded. I could not remember ever hearing this before at church. Perhaps I was just not in the right places, but for me I was awestruck, surprised, and a bit chagrined that no man had ever told me these things. And as I looked at the church around me, and even at my own life, I was not sure that these things could be true. I did not have complete victory over sin in my life, and I frankly did not believe it was possible to have it. If this is where you are, then this important portion of the book is for you.

It is true that Jesus came to earth to redeem mankind. He completely paid for our sins through his blood on the cross. It is also true that this redemption brought us back into relationship with God. Isaiah 59:2 says that our iniquities have separated us from our god and that our sins have hidden his face from us so that he will not hear us. So his redemption, paying for our sins, brought us back into relationship with God, and he now listens to us. This is called atonement.

**To Live Victoriously**

Jesus also saved us. As mentioned before, God's purpose in Christ was to save us from our sins, not in them. He set us free from the bondage of sin (John 8:34–36; Romans 6:16–22; Romans 8:2–4; 1 John 3:9) by defeating Satan, sin, and death on the cross. This salvation was completed at Christ's death and resurrection. We are saved by grace through faith in the completed work of Jesus Christ. The problem, therefore, is not salvation.

The problem is *staying* saved and reconciled. The problem is not that we have been reconciled with God, but how do we stay reconciled and how do we remain victorious over sin, Satan, and death. The answer to these questions lies in a righteous view of eternal security, a spiritual understanding of "works" and the empowerment of God.

So many have bought into the popular concept of "Once saved, always saved." They've been taught that once they say the prayer or get baptized or speak in tongues or exercise some other denominational formulary, they will be perpetually saved no matter how much they sin or depart from the paths of God. This has caused many seekers to become weak or clever. "Anyway, I go to church, and that's better than most of my other friends. God should be proud of me." "I even tithe, and that is surely better than most." Perhaps they're thinking, "I wonder what is the cheapest insurance policy that I can buy and still get into heaven. I guess I could listen to the gospel and say a five-minute prayer if that's all it takes."

The problem with such thinking is that God is not mocked. He knows what we're thinking. He knows why we do things.

> But they mocked the messengers of God, despised His words, and scoffed at His prophets, until the wrath of the LORD arose against His people, till there was no remedy.
>
> 2 CHRONICLES 36:16 (NKJV)

> Do not be deceived, God is not mocked; for whatever a man sows, that he will also reap.
>
> Galatians 6:7 (NKJV)

> For I know their works and their thoughts. It shall be that I will gather all nations and tongues; and they shall come and see My glory.
>
> Isaiah 66:18 (NKJV)

Furthermore, contrary to the popular theological teachings of today, it *is* possible to lose one's salvation. The Word of God states both directly and indirectly that the Christian can lose his or her salvation. The following are samples of such scriptures:

> I am the true vine, and My Father is the vinedresser. Every branch in Me that does not bear fruit He takes away; and every branch that bears fruit He prunes, that it may bear more fruit. You are already clean because of the word which I have spoken to you. Abide in Me, and I in you. As the branch cannot bear fruit of itself, unless it abides in the vine, neither can you, unless you abide in Me. I am the vine, you are the branches. He who abides in Me, and I in him, bears much fruit; for without Me you can do nothing. If anyone does not abide in Me, he is cast out as a branch and is withered; and they gather them and throw them into the fire, and they are burned.
>
> John 15:1–6 (NKJV)

As mentioned earlier, everyone who is in Christ is a member of his body, the church. He is a Christian. Here it says that every branch in Christ that does not remain in him is cast out, withered, thrown into the fire, and burned. Obviously, Jesus believes that there's a possibility that people will deny him even after becoming Christians and leave him. The reference to being thrown into the fire and burned does not conjure up the idea of staying saved.

> For I speak to you Gentiles; inasmuch as I am an apostle to the Gentiles, I magnify my ministry, if by any means I may provoke to jealousy those who are my flesh and save some of them. For if their being cast away is the reconciling of the world, what will their acceptance be but life from the dead? For if the first fruit is holy, the lump is also holy; and if the root is holy, so are the branches. And if some of the branches were broken off, and you, being a wild olive tree, were grafted in among them, and with them became a partaker of the root and fatness of the olive tree, do not boast against the branches. But if you do boast, remember that you do not support the root, but the root supports you. You will say then, "Branches were broken off that I might be grafted in." Well said. Because of unbelief they were broken off, and you stand by faith. Do not be haughty, but fear. *For if God did not spare the natural branches, He may not spare you either.* Therefore consider the goodness and severity of God: on those who fell, severity; but toward you, goodness, *if you continue in His goodness. Otherwise you also will be cut off. And they also, if they do not continue in unbelief, will be grafted in, for God is able to graft them in again.*
>
> ROMANS 11:13–23 (NKJV, ITALICS MINE)

In this passage, Paul is obviously talking to the Gentile Christian Romans about the state of Jewish nonbelievers. They were cut off from the Root, Jesus Christ. But he is cautioning them not to become proud now that they are the favored ones, but to fear. Why? Because if they do not continue in the way of Christ, they also will be cut off. And they are Christian believers.

> For it is impossible for those who were once enlightened, and have tasted the heavenly gift, and have become partakers of the Holy Spirit, and have tasted the good word of God and the powers of the age to come, if they fall away, to renew them again to repentance, since they crucify again for themselves the Son of God, and put Him to an open shame. For the earth which drinks in the rain that often comes upon it, and bears herbs useful for those by whom it is cultivated, receives

> blessing from God; but if it bears thorns and briars, it is rejected and near to being cursed, whose end is to be burned.
>
> Hebrews 6:4–8 (NKJV)

These verses refer to mature Christians—ones who have been enlightened, have tasted the gifts of God, have been filled with the Holy Spirit, have read the Scriptures, and have witnessed at least some of the power of God. If these people fall away, it is impossible to renew them to repentance. Their end is to be burned.

Remember, to whom the Lord has given much, of him is the more required (Luke 12:48). He has given his Son, his Spirit, and his Word to all Christians. Therefore, he requires more from his followers than mental assent to his existence and vain worship in the churches (Isaiah 1:12–17).

Now consider the following verse as it relates to "works":

> And to the angel of the church in Sardis write, "These things says He who has the seven Spirits of God and the seven stars: I know your works, that you have a name that you are alive, but you are dead. Be watchful, and strengthen the things which remain, that are ready to die, for I have not found your works perfect before God. Remember therefore how you have received and heard; hold fast and repent. Therefore if you will not watch, I will come upon you as a thief, and you will not know what hour I will come upon you. You have a few names even in Sardis who have not defiled their garments; and they shall walk with Me in white, for they are worthy. He who overcomes shall be clothed in white garments, and I will not blot out his name from the Book of Life; but I will confess his name before My Father and before His angels. He who has an ear, let him hear what the Spirit says to the churches."
>
> Revelation 3:1–6 (NKJV)

Notice that when Jesus addresses the church at Sardis, he says that there are a few in the church who have not defiled their garments, presumably because of some sin. There are a few whose names he would not blot out of the Book of Life. The implication is that there are many Christians in the church whose names he will blot out of the Book of Life, who will not be saved. In fact, to all seven of the churches to whom Jesus addresses his comments in Revelation, he states in the end "to him who overcomes." The criteria for blessing in every case is overcoming until the end—finishing the race, not just beginning. It's godly behavior, not just a proper theology (James 1:21–22). It's walking as Jesus walked (1 John 2:6), not just saying the prayer. Revelation 2:23 says as much: "I will kill her children with death, and all the churches shall know that I am He who searches the minds and hearts. And I will give to each one of you according to your works" (NKJV).

Now I know that some of you, readers, may be uncomfortable with the scriptures above on two counts: (1) the teachings you received on eternal security and (2) the teachings you received on works righteousness. Let's look briefly at each.

The verses most frequently quoted for eternal security are the following:

> My sheep hear My voice, and I know them, and they follow Me. And I give them eternal life, and they shall never perish; neither shall anyone snatch them out of My hand. My Father, who has given them to Me, is greater than all; and no one is able to snatch them out of My Father's hand.
>
> John 10:27–29 (NKJV)

> This is the will of the Father who sent Me, that of all He has given Me I should lose nothing, but should raise it up at the last day. And this is the will of Him who sent Me, that everyone who sees the Son and believes in Him may have everlasting life; and I will raise him up at the last day.
>
> John 6:39–40 (NKJV)

> And this is the testimony: that God has given us eternal life, and this life is in His Son. He who has the Son has life; he who does not have the Son of God does not have life. These things I have written to you who believe in the name of the Son of God, that you may know that you have eternal life, and that you may continue to believe in the name of the Son of God.
>
> 1 John 5:11–13 (NKJV)

> For God so loved the world that He gave His only begotten Son, that whoever believes in Him should not perish but have everlasting life.
>
> John 3:16 (NKJV)

> Blessed be the God and Father of our Lord Jesus Christ, who has blessed us with every spiritual blessing in the heavenly places in Christ, just as He chose us in Him before the foundation of the world, that we should be holy and without blame before Him in love, having predestined us to adoption as sons by Jesus Christ to Himself, according to the good pleasure of His will, to the praise of the glory of His grace, by which He has made us accepted in the Beloved. In Him we have redemption through His blood, the forgiveness of sins, according to the riches of His grace.
>
> Ephesians 1:3–7 (NKJV)

Beloved, these are truly beautiful and wonderful promises for those of us who are in Christ Jesus, i.e., for those who are in the church, which is his body. The great Christian joy is that we do have security in Christ Jesus. No one can snatch us out of his hand. Satan can't, the world can't, your employer can't, your government can't, your wife or children can't—no one can. No one, that is, except you. God will not force you to be saved or to stay saved. You have the right to invite Jesus Christ into your life, and you have the right to reject him and send him out. So losing your salvation is possible, and it is your choice. By rejecting his word and his rule in your life, you reject him as your King (Lord) and Savior and send him out.

Those who cling to election or predestination, or the sovereignty of God in the area of salvation, should look at Ephesians 1 carefully. As Paul and others have perspicaciously and repeatedly shown, all of the promises and blessings noted are "*in* Christ Jesus." Try underlining each passage in the New testament that contains the words "*in* Christ," "*in* Him," "*in* the Beloved," "*in* Whom" (when referring to Jesus), and then meditate about what the passage is claiming about being in that position. You'll be amazed at the centrality of that issue in Christianity. All our spiritual blessings, election, predestination, acceptance, redemption, forgiveness, unity, inheritance, etc., are "*in* Christ Jesus." Furthermore, "*all promises of God in Him are Yes, and in Him Amen, to the glory of God through us*" (2 Corinthians 1:20, NKJV, italics mine). So all of our spiritual blessings are in the church, which is Christ's body. When we are *in* him, we are saved. When we depart from him, we're not. Election is for those who are called into covenant relationship with God, which for Christians means the new covenant of communion in Christ (John 6:53–57; Luke 22:19–20). Further, the predestination of all believers is to be conformed to the image of Christ (Romans 8:29). Therefore anytime a Christian rejects Christ as his Master and Savior, he loses his election and predestination since both are *in* Christ (Ephesians 1:3–13).

Having said all this, I would like to quote Hebrews:

> But, beloved, we are confident of better things concerning you, yes, things that accompany salvation, though we speak in this manner. For God is not unjust to forget your work and labor of love which you have shown toward His name, in that you have ministered to the saints, and do minister. And we desire that each one of you show the same diligence to the full assurance of hope until the end, that you do not

> become sluggish, but imitate those who through faith and patience inherit the promises.
>
> HEBREWS 6:9–12 (NKJV)

Now let's return to the most serious obstruction to perfection facing man: sin. If God had not decided to empower man to have victory over sin, then the work of Jesus Christ on the cross would have been like setting Adam and Eve back in the garden, only to let them be tempted again and fall. For although God had reconciled man to himself and washed him in the blood of Christ, there still remained another critical issue. How was man going to maintain that reconciliation and that spotless justification? What would prevent him from committing the same mistakes that he had made for thousands of years, thus plunging himself back into darkness and separation from God?

The answer to that question reveals the absolute genius and love of God. He clearly understood the issue. His chosen people, the natural descendants of Abraham, Isaac, and Jacob, had received God's laws and statutes by the hands of Moses. They understood the laws and entered into a covenant relationship with God concerning them. The problem was that the commands were written on tablets of stone or on scrolls. When they were out of sight, they were out of mind. And although prophets came and went, reminding the people of their promises to obey, they were nevertheless unable or unwilling to consistently follow God's rules. They demonstrated repeatedly that mankind is incapable on his own to scrupulously remember God's laws and obey them, even with the motivation of great reward if they did. External laws and promises were not strong enough to overcome the lusts and temptations of the flesh and implement consistently righteous and holy behavior in man.

## To Comprehend and Live in the New-Covenant Paradigm

In light of all this, God's master plan from the beginning was not only to send his Son to save mankind but also to send his own Spirit into man to empower him to stay saved and victorious, i.e., to keep his laws and to do his will. Once again, carefully consider the implications of the following powerful revelations of God:

> I will give you a new heart and put a new spirit within you; I will take the heart of stone out of your flesh and give you a heart of flesh. I will put My Spirit within you and *cause* you to walk in My statutes, and you will keep My judgments and do them.
>
> Ezekiel 36:26–27 (NKJV, italics mine)

> But this is the covenant that I will make with the house of Israel after those days, says the LORD: I will put My law in their minds, and write it on their hearts; and I will be their God, and they shall be My people. No more shall every man teach his neighbor, and every man his brother, saying, "Know the LORD," for they all shall know Me, from the least of them to the greatest of them, says the LORD. For I will forgive their iniquity, and their sin I will remember no more.
>
> Jeremiah 31:33–34 (NKJV)

> There is therefore now no condemnation to those who are in Christ Jesus, who do not walk according to the flesh, but according to the Spirit. For the law of the Spirit of life in Christ Jesus has made me free from the law of sin and death. For what the law could not do in that it was weak through the flesh, God did by sending His own Son in the likeness of sinful flesh, on account of sin: *He condemned sin in the flesh, that the righteous requirement of the law might be fulfilled in us who do not walk according to the flesh but according to the Spirit.*
>
> Romans 8:1–4 (NKJV, italics mine)

> Whoever commits sin also commits lawlessness, and sin is lawlessness. And you know that He was manifested to take away our sins, and

> in Him there is no sin. Whoever abides in Him does not sin. Whoever sins has neither seen Him nor known Him. Little children, let no one deceive you. He who practices righteousness is righteous, just as He is righteous. He who sins is of the devil, for the devil has sinned from the beginning. For this purpose the Son of God was manifested, that He might destroy the works of the devil. *Whoever has been born of God does not sin, for His seed remains in him; and he cannot sin, because he has been born of God.*
>
> 1 JOHN 3:4–9 (NKJV, ITALICS MINE)

> No temptation has overtaken you except such as is common to man; but God is faithful, who will not allow you to be tempted beyond what you are able, but with the temptation will also make the way of escape, that you may be able to bear it.
>
> 1 CORINTHIANS 10:13 (NKJV)

> We know that *whoever is born of God does not sin*; but he who has been born of God keeps himself, and the wicked one does not touch him.
>
> 1 JOHN 5:18 (NKJV, ITALICS MINE)

Wow! Amazing verses, aren't they? One would do well to read them repeatedly so that they might sink into one's mind and heart.

Although these verses are pretty self-explanatory, I would like to make a few comments about each of them. The Ezekiel passage has been referenced already with regard to its impact on our having a new heart. Here, however, I would like to draw your attention to God's promise to put into us his Holy Spirit. What an awesome promise! And it has already been fulfilled in all born-again Christians.

> Do you not know that you are the temple of God and that the Spirit of God dwells in you?
>
> 1 CORINTHIANS 3:16 (NKJV)

> Or do you not know that your body is the temple of the Holy Spirit who is in you, whom you have from God, and you are not your own?
>
> 1 CORINTHIANS 6:19 (NKJV)

The fact that the Holy Spirit dwells in all Christians must be established and understood before the full impact of the second portion of the Ezekiel verses above can be felt. For the very purpose that God places his Holy Spirit in us, according to verse 27, is to empower (lit. cause) man to obey his laws and to keep and do his judgments.

For years the church has ignored this primary purpose of the Holy Spirit. They have preferred to focus on the gifts and the fruits, marveling at healings, tongues, slayings, exorcisms, prophecies, etc. While all these are awesome and beautiful demonstrations of the power of the Holy Spirit, none of them gets to the root cause of righteousness and holiness, which is God's primary purpose for saving mankind. We are straining at the gnat and swallowing the camel (Matthew 23:24). Sin is the greatest problem mankind has! And in this passage, God is showing us that he has dealt with that problem. God in Christ has triumphed over sin, and through the Holy Spirit he has now enabled us to be triumphant over sin also. Praise God! This is truly good news. Notice how the Spirit confirms this triumphant nature in Christ:

> Now thanks be to God who always leads us in triumph in Christ, and through us diffuses the fragrance of His knowledge in every place.
>
> 2 CORINTHIANS 2:14 (NKJV)

The advent of the new covenant, the essence of which is explained in Jeremiah 31 and following, was not just some future promise. It was confirmed by Jesus and sealed at the Last Supper (cf. Matthew 26:26–28, etc.). It is further detailed in the book of Hebrews 8–10. This new covenant is God's agreement with mankind now, not at some unspecified future date. The most salient point of this covenant, for purposes of our discussion on perfection, is the fact that God has now written his laws on our hearts. They are no longer on a tablet of stone, on some wall, or merely in the Bible. They're written in our hearts and minds by the Holy Spirit so that we can no longer say, "Out of sight, out of mind." But even more importantly, when thus written, they affect the very seat of our emotions so that the commandments are no longer a burden to us. They're our delight! We no longer *have* to keep the commandments: we *want* to! This is the paradigm shift of being born again. This is what changes our attitudes and our worldview. And this is the telltale mark of knowing Jesus Christ. Consider the following:

> By this we know that we love the children of God, when we love God and keep His commandments. For this is the love of God, that we keep His commandments. And His commandments are not burdensome. For whatever is born of God overcomes the world. And this is the victory that has overcome the world—our faith.
>
> 1 JOHN 5:2–4 (NKJV)

> But whoever keeps His word, truly the love of God is perfected in him. By this we know that we are in Him. He who says he abides in Him ought himself also to walk just as He walked.
>
> 1 JOHN 2:5–6 (NKJV)

## To Win the War between the Law of God and the Law of Sin

As detailed earlier, Romans 7 reveals the problem with having an intellectual faith in Christ and adds yet another dimension to this great victory over sin. It confirms that knowledge of Jesus and even a sincere desire to follow him and obey his laws are not enough to empower a person to live a victorious life as a Christian. Instead, we don't do the things we want to do, and we do the things we don't want to do! Maybe you've been there too! I have! In verses 21 to 23 Paul, by the Spirit, outlines the problem: "I find then a law, that, when I would do good, evil is present with me. For I delight in the *law of God* after the inward man; but I see *another law* in my members, warring against the law of my mind, and bringing me into captivity to the *law of sin* which is in my members" (italics mine).

He concludes in verse 24 with the following: "Oh, wretched man that I am! Who will deliver me from this body of death?"

Does this seem like the victorious Christian life to you? Yet, in truth, it does describe the conundrum of all who seek to follow Christ through study and human effort. It reveals the status of many who go to church and call themselves Christians but daily face the reality of living defeated lives when it comes to sin.

Clearly Paul wrote this passage after conversion, since he is writing to the Roman church after being sent as an apostle to the Gentiles. But the point of the discourse in this pericope centers specifically on the war between the law of God and the law of sin in verses 21 to 23. In chapter 7, the law of sin wins, demonstrating that it is not possible to overcome Satan and sin through human effort alone. The result of such human effort is, "Oh, wretched man that I am, who will deliver me from this body of death?" We Christians often forget that we cannot do it ourselves and that Christ warned us about this: "I am the vine, you are the branches. He who abides in Me, and I in him, bears much fruit; for without Me you can do nothing" (John 15:5, NKJV).

This is why we desperately need Christ in us through his Holy Spirit. Romans 8 follows man's defeat in chapter 7 with the glorious victory of the Holy Spirit in Romans 8:1–4. Note that life in Christ Jesus, the law of the Holy Spirit (God), sets us free from the law of sin and death! Praise God! Further, perusal of verses 3 and 4 confirms that the law was weak, unable to change hearts and motives, because of our fleshly nature. But God saw the problem and sent his Son in the likeness of sinful flesh to solve the problem of sin and condemn sin in the flesh. Why? So that the righteousness of the law might be fulfilled in us who walk in accordance with the Holy Spirit (cf. Matt 5:17).

Therefore, the specific purpose of Christ's victory over sin on the cross was to enable us to be redeemed and reconciled to God and then, through the Holy Spirit, to be able to walk victoriously in righteousness and holiness all the days of our life. It was to enable us to run the race and overcome until the end. This is his perfect plan for transforming a sinner into the "perfect" or "mature" man referenced in Ephesians 4:13. Praise God for this ingenious and loving plan!

**To Appropriate the Power of God's "Seed"**

All of this brings us now to a consideration of what I believe to be the most powerful prorighteousness passage in all of the scriptures: 1 John 3:4–9. John, by the Holy Spirit, brings us first to a definition of sin, which he characterizes as "the transgression of the law." This lawlessness is an attitude that places self and self-gratification on the throne of one's life. External laws of man or of God matter little to this person. He or she, through self-assertiveness and/or pride, has the audacity to feel in his or her heart: "I'm going to do what I want to do when I want to do it, and no one can tell me what to do or not to do." This is the spirit that rebels against the authority of God in their lives. It is the distilled essence of what the Bible calls the "old man" (e.g., Romans 6:6).

After defining sin, John affirms that Jesus came to take away our sins and that in him is no sin. Notice that "in him" is no sin. Now this is not surprising when referring to Jesus, since the Bible over and over proclaims his sinlessness (e.g., Hebrews 4:14–15). However, when "in him" is the formulary for the church or an individual Christian, the statement becomes profound and challenging. The immediately following context confirms that this latter nuance is the one intended (1 John 3:6): "Whosoever abides in Him [Jesus] does not sin, and whoever does sin has never seen Him nor known Him." Wow!

And if that's not challenging enough, consider the meat in verses 8 and 9 that follow. Here John is reminding the reader that one of the purposes of God in sending Jesus Christ to earth was to destroy the works of the devil, i.e., sin. Most Christians are aware that Jesus Christ has washed away their sins by his blood on the cross. Few, however, seem to be aware of the important function of the Holy Spirit in giving new birth to Christians and giving them the power not to sin. Verse 9, however, powerfully makes this statement. If you are a born-again Christian, you do not sin because God's seed (the Spirit of Christ, Romans 8:9) remains in you, and you cannot sin. It is a simple, straightforward statement, which comes to the complacent Christian like a right hook out of nowhere and lands right where we live. For most of us, it's a knockdown punch. Our first reaction usually is, "Where did that come from?" or "You've got to be joking," or "This must be some sort of mistranslation."

I admit that these were some of my own reactions when I first saw and pondered these verses. I was troubled about the implications for many years. I had been in leadership in my church, been on many short-term missions to Haiti, and been in small groups and Bible studies. Through all of these I had not known a single Christian who claimed victory over sin or even one that felt that sinlessness was a legitimate or attainable goal!

Consequently, when God called me into vocational ministry through a nighttime dream and a work-related miracle, the first thing I did was to resign my command at an Air Force reserve unit and enroll in a local seminary. I continued to operate a small business to maintain my family income and send my youngest son to college. At the seminary, I took up these verses and looked at them critically for a theology paper. It was in doing so that I made the discovery that the translation in the King James Version was not only correct, but the original language was also even stronger.

As mentioned in the preface, when the implications of these verses first dawned on me, I tried to discover a way to get around the clear meaning of this text. In light of my experience, and the church as I viewed it, it just didn't seem possible that God intended Christians to be sinless. All the churches I had attended had been emphasizing the finished work of Christ, God's grace, assurance of salvation, confession, and repentance. None had mentioned that a born-again Christian could not sin. Therefore I delved into the wording and grammar in the original Greek texts, looking for possible loopholes. The more I searched, the more I was convinced that the text meant exactly what it said. The Greek verb *poieo* (ποιέω[2]) means "to do" and is used to describe a single act, not something done repeatedly or continuously as in the durative sense of the Greek present tense rendered in the NIV thought-for-thought translation. According to Strong's concordance, the Greek verb *prasso* (πράσσω) is to be used as the verb "to do" in repetitive or continuous cases.[3] The verb used here, however, is *poiei.*[4] The word that is translated *sin, hamartian* (ἁμαρτίαν),[5] in verse 9a above, is a noun in the accusative, not a present-tense verb or infinitive as it is "dynamically" translated in the NIV. The literal translation from the Greek, therefore, is "Everyone who has been born out of the God does not do a sin because his sperm [seed] remains [lives, abides] in him and he is unable [cannot, does not have the power] to sin because he has been born out of the God." In plain English, the verse says that the born-again Christian does not commit a sin because God's seed (Jesus, the Holy Spirit of Christ) lives in him and won't allow him to sin. Wow! What an awesome blessing!

The implications of this truth are astounding. We literally have God as our spiritual Father when we're born again. And just the smallest "sperm" of the Spirit of his Son creates in us a whole new worldview. We are a new creation, the old has passed away, and all things have become new (2 Corinthians 5:17). We are literally "wired" to do the things that God has before ordained that we should walk in (Ephesians 2:10). We have the genetic propensity for righteousness and holiness and the genetic aversion to sin and wickedness, just like our Father. This reality, coupled with the unmerited gift of salvation by grace through faith in Jesus Christ, empowers a born-again Christian to live a godly life and attain the goals specified in Ephesians 4:13, i.e., the ability to attain the stature of the perfect, Christlike man.

The truth, therefore, is that God was not joking about perfection, and that the KJV rendering of 1 John 3:9 is not a mistranslation. Jesus said, "Be ye therefore perfect even as your father in heaven is perfect" (Matthew 5:48). Since the word proclaims that all have sinned and fallen short of the glory of God (Romans 3:23), if God had not provided a way to attain the perfection he commands, then we would be, of all people, the most frustrated and downhearted. But the fact is that he provided us with both the ability and the will to be sinless. The indwelling Holy Spirit is his means of empowering people to accomplish this feat.

## To Grasp the Way of Escape from Temptation

Turning now to 1 Corinthians 10:13, we find that God has silenced yet another objection to perfection, and that is the issue of temptation. Jesus himself noted that the "spirit is willing, but the flesh is weak." Many people take comfort in this all too obvious revelation. They're happy to think that "well anyway, Jesus understands my problem; I'm just weak in the flesh." Others fall back on 1 John 1:8–10, especially verse 9, forgetting that John also wrote 1 John 3:9 and 1 John 5:18, just two and four chapters later in the same letter, and that repentance must follow confession. Still others take comfort in Romans 7:14–24, hoping that somehow this description of a person's fleshly struggle with the law of God warring against the law of sin, and sin winning, legitimizes their errant behavior. We somehow think that it's all right to fall into sin if we're tempted beyond what we can handle or if "everybody's doing it, even my Christian friends."

Well, this passage clearly debunks this reasoning. The verse states that any temptation we get is something others have also experienced. We cannot say, "No one has been tempted as I have," or "Jesus does not understand my problem." This verse states that there is *no* temptation that we have experienced that is unique. Further, it asserts that *God* is faithful and will not allow us to be tempted more than what we can handle. God himself will make a way to escape the temptation so that we will not fall into sin. What a blessing!

But "how do I know that God can give me the power to overcome my temptations"? Because he gave that power to his Son Jesus, and now, through regeneration, he has given it to each one of us.

Consider a minute. What happened right after Jesus's baptism by John and the anointing of the Holy Spirit at the end of Matthew 3? The Holy Spirit led Jesus out into the wilderness to be tempted by Satan. God led him there! Think about that. The Bible says in the book of James that God tempts no man (James 1:13). So why would he subject his own Son to the most brutal testing ever? Satan offered Jesus all the glory and the power of the kingdoms of this world (Matthew 4:8–9). Jesus turned down the offer, preferring to serve and honor God alone. If God gave that power and will to his only begotten Son, can he not also do it for his adopted sons who have been regenerated by his Holy Spirit? The Bible says in Hebrews 4:15 that Jesus was tempted in every point just as we are, and he did not sin. We are the adopted children of God, and this same Spirit of Christ dwells in us. Therefore, the statement by Paul that God will not allow us to be tempted more than we can handle makes sense, not because we can persevere through self-will into righteousness (we cannot!) but because the indwelling Spirit of God empowers us to overcome temptation and live righteously.

Don't think that because we have this wonderful gift, Satan will never tempt us and that God will never test us. There's a good reason why Jesus instructed his disciples to pray, "Lead us not into temptation, but deliver us from the evil one." God may test us so that we might know what is in our own hearts and so that we might know the character and the godly strength that he has placed within us. It is also at these times of testing that we may discover our weaknesses and sins because of our failure to yield to the promptings and will of his Spirit. There'll be more on this issue when we consider the purposes of God in man.

**To Engage the Three Foundational Truths**

Finally, we come to a brief consideration of 1 John 5:18–20. This passage confirms three things that all Spirit-filled Christians "know."

> We know that whoever is born of God does not sin; but he who has been born of God keeps himself, and the wicked one does not touch him. We know that we are of God, and the whole world lies under the sway of the wicked one. And we know that the Son of God has come and has given us an understanding, that we may know Him who is true; and we are in Him who is true, in His Son Jesus Christ. This is the true God and eternal life.
>
> 1 JOHN 5:18–20 (NKJV)

First, we *know* that whoever has been born of God does not sin. Why? Because he "keeps himself" (keeps himself under guard, keeps himself in custody, keeps himself back[6]) from it. This is the second confirmation in this letter that born-again Christians do not sin because of the self-control given them by the Holy Spirit. Further, please note carefully that the result of this Spirit-empowered self-control is that the wicked one, Satan, does not touch him. Praise God!

One important cautionary note must be made here. At least one denomination has used this as a proof text that no Pentecostal Christian can be touched by Satan or demonized. These Christians assume everyone who speaks in tongues, or who has manifested a spiritual gift, qualifies for the blessings of this passage. But that is not what John, by the Spirit, is saying here. The specific manifestation of the Spirit mentioned here that qualifies the Christian for exemption from attacks of the wicked one is victory over sin. I have personally witnessed a Pentecostal seminary student manifest a demon while I was preaching. In a brief counseling session later, the student admitted that after he had backslidden, he had been afflicted. Willful sin opens the door to the evil one for anyone. Hebrews 10:26–31 is a stark warning and reminder of this fact.

Second, we *know* that we are of God and that the whole world lies in wickedness. The first affirmation is a wonderful joy; the second is obvious and heartbreaking to all who watch today's news. It's heartbreaking because it need not be so. The kingdom of God has come and is available to all who would seek and receive Jesus Christ on his terms. As simplistic as it may seem to some, Jesus Christ is the answer for all of the world's ills, and he is the hope of all mankind for a world filled with righteousness, justice, and love.

Third, we *know* that the Son of God has come and that he has given us an understanding (the mind of Christ) so that we may know the truth, and we are in the truth, in his Son, Jesus Christ (John 14:6). This is the true god and the everlasting life. Note that Jesus has given us his Mind so that we might know the Truth (him) and know that we are in the Truth (him). Further, when we're in the Truth, we have eternal life (cf. 1 John 5:11–12).

These are three foundational truths that John incorporates at the end of his first letter. They are summary issues. Mark carefully in your heart that all of these vitally important understandings are dependent on the empowerment of the Holy Spirit to give us the supernatural mind to know them.

## Summary

Beloved, our dear Lord knew through foreknowledge and historical experience that man's sinful nature was his Achilles' heel. Though many wanted to follow God, and some succeeded for long periods of time, none succeeded in living a consistently righteous life in this world. If history shows anything, it's that man's heart is desperately wicked and that religions extolling human effort or man-made idols failed to impart righteousness to the people exercised by them. This is why the first and primary purpose of God in sending his Holy Spirit to man was to empower man to have victory over sin and his sinful nature. This monumental task required a complete makeover of every person who would sincerely seek to follow Jesus Christ. It required a new birth, a new heart, a new parent, a new citizenship, and a new mind. All of these were graciously and powerfully imparted to the disciples at Pentecost and to each succeeding generation who sincerely sought to know Jesus Christ and to walk as he walked.

Therefore, our emphasis in the churches must not be on man's wisdom, reason, or rhetorical excellence. What people are really looking for today is the demonstration of the Holy Spirit and of power in the church. And what greater demonstration of both than that a man or woman walk as Jesus walked in holiness, righteousness, and unselfish love? When people see the evidence of a changed and holy life, they know that this is not window dressing: this is the genuine work of the power of God! Our homes and fellowships will be transformed. The outward trappings of human excellence will vanish in the Shechinah glory of the Spirit-filled and empowered church that worships and walks in the Spirit and in the truth.

## Teach and Guide Man into All Truth

God is well aware of man's need to know the truth. No man can make wise decisions based on faulty premises. The problem for man is that he is wildly adrift on a sea of relativity: what's true for Ghana may not be true for Russia, what's true in Japan may be alien to Britain, what's culturally acceptable in America may be an insult in Thailand, and what is commonly practiced in Saudi Arabia may be shocking in the jungles of the Amazon. The plethora of philosophies, governments, religions, cultures, ethics, and morals has made it difficult for humans to agree on what is "true," "right," or "good" in many areas of life. When one adds pride and lust to this milieu, one quickly discovers the rudiments of hatred, strife, envy, discontent, distrust, and, ultimately, war.

The world can no longer afford the flippant response of Pontius Pilate, "What is truth?" (John 18:38). The fact is that we desperately need to know the truth. We need to know that there is a standard. We need to know there is a supreme lawgiver. We need to know that there is a transnational, transcultural, and transcendent truth. But for some perverse reason, man continues to look to other men to solve his problems, dictate his laws, manage his family, and set standards for his children. It's like one computer asking another computer to solve its problems rather than going to the one who designed the computer and asking him how the hardware and software were designed to run on the machine and how it can be fixed so that it will run most efficiently and harmoniously within the network of other computers.

### Confirm the Truth of God's Creation

God is our creator. He knows how we work. He knows the truth of every system and subsystem in our body and how each is programmed to work harmoniously in conjunction with other humans with similar systems and subsystems, and, additionally, with other human and nonhuman systems and subsystems in an interdependent network.

Therefore, knowing our human limitations, God sent his Son, who is the Truth (John 14:6), and his Holy Spirit, who is the Spirit of truth (John 14:17), that man might know the truth and that the truth would set him free (John 8:32, 36). Of particular note here is the Holy Spirit's part in conveying truth to man delineated in the following verses:

> And I will pray the Father, and He will give you another Helper, that He may abide with you forever—the Spirit of truth, whom the world cannot receive, because it neither sees Him nor knows Him; but you know Him, for He dwells with you and will be in you.
>
> John 14:16–17 (NKJV)

> But the Helper, the Holy Spirit, whom the Father will send in My name, He will teach you all things, and bring to your remembrance all things that I said to you.
>
> John 14:26 (NKJV)

> But when the Helper comes, whom I shall send to you from the Father, the Spirit of truth who proceeds from the Father, He will testify of Me.
>
> John 15:26 (NKJV)

> However, when He, the Spirit of truth, has come, He will guide you into all truth; for He will not speak on His own authority, but whatever He hears He will speak; and He will tell you things to come. He will glorify Me, for He will take of what is Mine and declare it to you.
>
> John 16:13–14 (NKJV)

> But the anointing which you have received from Him abides in you, and you do not need that anyone teach you; but as the same anointing

teaches you concerning all things, and is true, and is not a lie, and just as it has taught you, you will abide in Him.

1 John 2:27 (NKJV)

From the above, it is clear that God has provided all Christians the ability to know the truth through his Spirit of truth. This Helper (Comforter, Counselor, Paraclete) is sent in Christ's name, proceeds from the Father, and lives in Christians. His job is to "guide us into all truth." How will he do that? By teaching us all things and bringing to our remembrance all things that Jesus said to us. What an awesome blessing! Therefore, since God is omniscient, there is nothing of the truth that the Spirit of truth cannot reveal to us. But note that the Spirit of truth will not speak on his own but will only convey what he is told to share from the Father. In this area, he's under the same constraints as Jesus was (John 12:49–50, 8:28). He is not a loose cannon, and he will not speak anything that contradicts what Christ or he himself has already spoken in the scriptures through the men he has inspired (2 Peter 1:15–21; 2 Timothy 3:16–4:4).

## Glorify Jesus and Testify of Him

Another distinguishing characteristic of the Holy Spirit of truth is that he glorifies Jesus and testifies of him. Therefore every Christian filled with the Holy Spirit will glorify Jesus and testify of the wonderful things that he has done in his or her life. And this is not something that he or she will do out of necessity or a feeling of obligation but because he or she wants to. Believe me, when you have been eyewitnesses of God's grace and power as Jackie and I have here, in Haiti, in the Philippines, and in other places in Asia, you will have no problem whatever in praising God and testifying of the things he has done and is doing. The most difficult part is not the witnessing but the indifference and unbelief that it often engenders in unbelievers, and even in many Christians. Nevertheless, when one's heart is full, it will naturally overflow when moved with the joy and testimony of what the Lord has done.

## Teach Believers the Truth

Last, but not least, 1 John 2:27 makes a profound statement about the ability of the Holy Spirit of truth to teach believers: "But the anointing which you have received from Him abides in you, and you do not need that anyone teach you." Why? Because *the Holy Spirit himself will teach you all things*. Further, he *is* the Truth and will teach you no lies. This is vitally important for the following expressed scriptural reasons:

> Now the Spirit expressly says that in latter times some will depart from the faith, giving heed to deceiving spirits and doctrines of demons, speaking lies in hypocrisy, having their own conscience seared with a hot iron.
>
> 1 TIMOTHY 4:1–2 (NKJV)

> I charge you therefore before God and the Lord Jesus Christ, who will judge the living and the dead at His appearing and His kingdom: Preach the word! Be ready in season and out of season. Convince, rebuke, exhort, with all longsuffering and teaching. For the time will come when they will not endure sound doctrine, but according to their own desires, because they have itching ears, they will heap up for themselves teachers; and they will turn their ears away from the truth, and be turned aside to fables.
>
> 2 TIMOTHY 4:1–4 (NKJV)

> But there were also false prophets among the people, even as there will be false teachers among you, who will secretly bring in destructive heresies, even denying the Lord who bought them, and bring on themselves swift destruction. And many will follow their destructive ways,

> because of whom the way of truth will be blasphemed. By covetousness they will exploit you with deceptive words; for a long time their judgment has not been idle, and their destruction does not slumber.
>
> 2 Peter 2:1–3 (NKJV)

> For false christs and false prophets will rise and show great signs and wonders to deceive, if possible, even the elect. See, I have told you beforehand.
>
> Matthew 24:24–25 (NKJV)

Dear ones, we live in an age of deception. It has become popular to distribute disinformation widely on the web and other media. The majority of people feel that it's acceptable to lie.[7] We have to resort to the likes of a Snopes.com to filter out rumors and untruths from circulating e-mails. The problem is who is monitoring these truth filters and their biases and interpretations of "truth"? Who is monitoring or controlling the news media? Or, closer to home, who is monitoring the denominations to test their doctrines and teachings and the spirit that is in them?

John, through the Spirit, warns us as follows:

> Beloved, do not believe every spirit, but test the spirits, whether they are of God; because many false prophets have gone out into the world. By this you know the Spirit of God: Every spirit that confesses that Jesus Christ has come in the flesh is of God [lit. Greek, "flesh, *out of the God*, is" (the Spirit of God)], and every spirit that does not confess that Jesus Christ has come in the flesh [lit. Greek, *out of the God*] is not of God. And this is the spirit of the Antichrist, which you have heard was coming, and is now already in the world. You are of God, little children, and have overcome them, because He who is in you is greater than he who is in the world.
>
> 1 John 4:1–4 (NKJV)

Notice that it is the Spirit of God in us that has overcome the false prophets, revealed to all born-again Christians the lies and deceptions of the evil one, and confirmed in our minds and hearts the truth from God. What joy and confidence this brings us! Knowing that there are absolute truths and standards, that there are laws that enable loving governance, and that there is a righteous and holy judge brings clarity and consistency to an often-confused world. To know that we need not be sucked into the maelstrom of philosophical musings, the whirlpool of situational ethics, the noose of political correctness, the cesspools of the proud and powerful, or the black holes of false religions is a joy unspeakable to those who understand that the wisdom of God is "first pure, then peaceable, gentle, easy to be entreated, full of mercy and good fruits, without partiality, and without hypocrisy" (James 3:17, KJV).

Jesus himself has said we shall know the truth and the truth shall set us free! (John 8:32) *He is The Truth* and, if he sets us free, we shall be free indeed (John 14:6, 8:36). "Free from what?" you may ask. From the context of the John 8 passages, it's sin! Happily, he and his Spirit also sets us free from many of sin's causes and effects, including confusion, deception, envy, strife, immorality, addiction, Satan, death, a bad conscience, hatred, jealousy, lust, bitterness, pride, hypocrisy, covetousness, and more.

Today, much of the world is held in bondage by lies and deceit. Satan, who is the father of lies (John 8:44), has bound billions of people in his web of spiritual darkness. The proliferation of cults and cultic practices and beliefs in the past two millennia is simply amazing. Many have been paralyzed by, addicted to, or culturally ensnared by such practices. The function of the Holy Spirit in this vital area is to anoint his people with truth so that they might carry on the work that Jesus began by bringing light and righteousness to the world and setting the captives free. Jesus put it this way:

> The Spirit of the LORD is upon Me, Because He has anointed Me To preach the gospel to the poor; He has sent Me to heal the broken-hearted, To proclaim liberty to the captives And recovery of sight to the blind, To set at liberty those who are oppressed; To proclaim the acceptable year of the LORD.
>
> Luke 4:18–19 (NKJV)

## Summary

The second major purpose of the Holy Spirit, then, is to teach and to guide all men into the truth. He, Jesus, and the Bible constitute the "plumb line" prophesied in Amos 7:7–8, which God uses to establish a firm foundation of truth in human relationships. Truth is the most powerful weapon against Satan and his minions. It sheds light in every dark corner and every private closet of man. It scatters deception and dispels the lie. Knowledge, wisdom, and understanding are built upon the foundation of truth. Therefore, whenever truth is perverted, twisted, or supplanted by hypocrisy, guile, deception, or lies, all our attempts to act wisely will also be distorted. That is why, in Paul's list of spiritual armor in Ephesians 6:12–17, truth is the girding of the Christian soldier's loins. It protects one's strength and the communications of life. It is also why the apostle John says that he has no greater joy than to hear that his children walk in the truth (3 John 4).

# Gift Man for Ministry

When we are born again, the Holy Spirit comes into us and gives each of us all of his fruits and at least one of his spiritual gifts. The spiritual gifts are given to individuals for the edification of the church and the glory of God. When each member utilizes his or her spiritual gift(s), then the church will operate harmoniously and powerfully as a single body, reflecting to the community and the world the multifaceted radiance of Christ. This is the way the church was designed by God to operate. Consider the following texts:

> Most assuredly, I say to you, he who believes in Me, the works that I do he will do also; and greater works than these he will do, because I go to My Father. And whatever you ask in My name, that I will do, that the Father may be glorified in the Son. If you ask anything in My name, I will do it.
>
> JOHN 14:12–14 (NKJV)

> And He said to them, "Go into all the world and preach the gospel to every creature. He who believes and is baptized will be saved; but he who does not believe will be condemned. And these signs will follow those who believe: In My name they will cast out demons; they will speak with new tongues; they will take up serpents; and if they drink anything deadly, it will by no means hurt them; they will lay hands on the sick, and they will recover." So then, after the Lord had spoken to them, He was received up into heaven, and sat down at the right hand of God. And they went out and preached everywhere, the Lord working with them and confirming the word through the accompanying signs. Amen.
>
> MARK 16:15–20 (NKJV)

> But the manifestation of the Spirit is given to each one for the profit of all: for to one is given the word of wisdom through the Spirit, to another the word of knowledge through the same Spirit, to another faith by the same Spirit, to another gifts of healings by the same Spirit,
> 10 to another the working of miracles, to another prophecy, to another discerning of spirits, to another different kinds of tongues, to another the interpretation of tongues. But one and the same Spirit works all these things, distributing to each one individually as He wills. For as

the body is one and has many members, but all the members of that one body, being many, are one body, so also is Christ. For by one Spirit we were all baptized into one body—whether Jews or Greeks, whether slaves or free—and have all been made to drink into one Spirit. For in fact the body is not one member but many. If the foot should say, "Because I am not a hand, I am not of the body," is it therefore not of the body? And if the ear should say, "Because I am not an eye, I am not of the body," is it therefore not of the body? If the whole body were an eye, where would be the hearing? If the whole were hearing, where would be the smelling? But now God has set the members, each one of them, in the body just as He pleased. And if they were all one member, where would the body be? But now indeed there are many members, yet one body. And the eye cannot say to the hand, "I have no need of you"; nor again the head to the feet, "I have no need of you." No, much rather, those members of the body which seem to be weaker are necessary. And those members of the body which we think to be less honorable, on these we bestow greater honor; and our unpresentable parts have greater modesty, but our presentable parts have no need. But God composed the body, having given greater honor to that part which lacks it, that there should be no schism in the body, but that the members should have the same care for one another. And if one member suffers, all the members suffer with it; or if one member is honored, all the members rejoice with it. Now you are the body of Christ, and members individually.

1 CORINTHIANS 12:7–27 (NKJV)

And He Himself gave some to be apostles, some prophets, some evangelists, and some pastors and teachers, for the equipping of the saints for the work of ministry, for the edifying of the body of Christ.

EPHESIANS 4:11–12 (NKJV)

But the fruit of the Spirit is love, joy, peace, longsuffering, kindness, goodness, faithfulness, gentleness, self-control. Against such there is no law.

GALATIANS 5:22–23 (NKJV)

## Why Spiritual Gifts?

It is not the purpose of this book to explicate the gifts or the fruits of the Spirit or to develop the nuances of meaning or application. Many other works have done that. Nevertheless, one of the primary purposes of the Holy Spirit is to provide his fruits and gifts to mankind so that, with character and power, believers might effectively bring the gospel of the kingdom of God to the world.

Therefore, it is within the scope of this book to prove God's intention to empower believers for righteous ministry. From the Gospel of John above, we see that it is not only Jesus's intent that believers would do the same works that he did but that they would also do even *greater ones*! This is astonishing! And note that he says "believers," not just apostles, prophets, evangelists, pastors, or teachers. The implications of this are astounding, and the fact that he was serious about his statement is clearly revealed in the history of the early Church and in the book of Acts. Many fellowships even today have experienced miracles of healing, casting out of demons, prophecy, people being raised from the dead, etc.

## Four Tests of Authenticity

The Mark passage above affirms God's intention to attest to the veracity of his word and the ministry of his believers by working with them and confirming their teachings by signs and wonders following them. God does not work miracles just to impress people with his power. He doesn't have to do that: his creation screams of his power, beauty, wisdom, and love (Romans 1:18–21). No, he uses signs and wonders to confirm his word, to give powerful proof that the teachings of the believer are truly from him.

However, because of Satan's multifaceted deceptions today, one must hasten to note that there are three other proofs necessary to evaluate the teachings of a true believer. Why? Because Christ has already warned us that in the last days, there will be many false christs who will do powerful signs and wonders to try to deceive even the elect (Matthew 24:23–25). John also echoes the warning and states that even at his time, many false prophets had already gone into the world (1 John 4:1).

Therefore, signs and wonders alone do not prove that a person is a loyal follower of Christ. Neither does the possession or use of other spiritual gifts prove one's Christianity. Followers of many of the world's religions speak in tongues, for example, and I and many others have also seen the evil one work "miracles" through cultic practices. So be careful if signs and wonders are the only proof that a person displays to demonstrate that he or she is a believer. To be sure, godly miracles were tools frequently used by Jesus to confirm his teachings and to attest to his identity as the Christ, but they were not the only proofs. There are other proofs that the Bible also gives for determining whether a believer is a true Christian teacher. The first of these is offered in the following statement of our Lord:

> Beware of false prophets, who come to you in sheep's clothing, but inwardly they are ravenous wolves. You will know them by their fruits. Do men gather grapes from thorn bushes or figs from thistles? Even so, every good tree bears good fruit, but a bad tree bears bad fruit. A good tree cannot bear bad fruit, nor can a bad tree bear good fruit. Every tree that does not bear good fruit is cut down and thrown into the fire. Therefore by their fruits you will know them. Not everyone who says to Me, "Lord, Lord," shall enter the kingdom of heaven, but he who does the will of My Father in heaven. Many will say to Me in that day, "Lord, Lord, have we not prophesied in Your name, cast out demons in Your name, and done many wonders in Your name?" And then I will declare to them, "I never knew you; depart from Me, you who practice lawlessness!"
>
> Matthew 7:15–23 (NKJV)

Two other proofs that person is a true Christian teacher, therefore, are that he or she *does the will of the Father* and that he or she manifests the fruits of the Holy Spirit and walks in the Spirit as referenced in Galatians 5:22–25. Indeed, a good tree cannot bear bad fruit. A mango tree cannot bear peaches. (Note James 3:12–18.) Jesus is the vine, and we are the branches. Jesus manifested the fruits of the Holy Spirit, and so should every Christian. The very "sap" of our lives flows from our root in Christ, and, as his branches, the fruit we bear ought to reflect the life and fruits of our Root. Just raising our hands in church and saying, "Lord, Lord," does not make us a Christian any more than swimming in the ocean makes us a fish. Neither does casting out demons alone prove that we're true Christians.

I want to hasten to say, however, that casting out demons is not a bad thing. In fact, it is a great blessing both for the person who is released from the bondage of demonic oppression or possession and for the one praying for the deliverance. I've had the privilege of being an eyewitness to several of God's deliverances, and in every case the relief on the faces of those afflicted was a joy to behold. And this is what Jesus says about those who participated in the intercession for the deliverance:

> Behold, I give you the authority to trample on serpents and scorpions, and over all the power of the enemy, and nothing shall by any means hurt you. Nevertheless do not rejoice in this, that the spirits are subject to you, but rather rejoice because your names are written in heaven.
>
> LUKE 10:19–20 (NKJV)

Praise God if your name is written in heaven! (cf. Revelation 20:15) And if you know it is, do not hesitate to use the gifts that God has given you for the edification of the church. Someone may even now be waiting for you to intercede for them to our Father. If you're not sure, then pray earnestly for God's guidance and assurance, remembering the seven sons of Sceva (Acts 19:13–17) who carelessly tried to cast out demons in the name of the "Jesus whom

Paul preaches" and were attacked, wounded, stripped, and thrown out themselves!

A fourth scriptural test of a true Christian teacher has already been mentioned earlier, i.e., the one referenced in 1 John 4:1–3. It states that any spirit who confesses that Jesus Christ has come in the flesh out of the God is the Spirit of God. Further, any spirit that does not confess that Jesus Christ is come in the flesh out of the God, i.e., that does not confess that Jesus is fully man and fully God is the spirit of Antichrist.

If a Christian teacher passes all four of these scriptural litmus tests, then it is safe to heed his or her instruction; if not, the listener must be very wary. The teacher may be very sincere and very well educated, but they may be as wrong as the scribes and the Pharisees were in the days of Jesus. In some cases, they may be actively trying to deceive and take people away from true Christianity into some watered-down form of it, or a cult. In these cases, the Scriptures must be the plumb line, not some subjective "the Holy Spirit told me that it was okay to be actively homosexual and divorced" or "I had a burning in my bosom testifying to the truth" (cf. 2 Timothy 3:16–17, etc.).

Teaching, however, is just one of the ministries given by the Holy Spirit. Many others have been highlighted in the verses above. Each has its important place in the church. And each saint imbued with his or her gift(s) has a vital mission for the Lord in the church and to the world. Consider carefully what Paul by the Spirit has written: "For we are His workmanship, created in Christ Jesus for good works, which God prepared beforehand that we should walk in them" (Ephesians 2:10, NKJV). Indeed, God does have a ministry plan for each believer's life, and that plan is important to him.

## Summary

In summary then, another major purpose of God in sending his Holy Spirit into each believer was to infuse him or her with godly character (the fruits) and abilities (the gifts). Each believer was to receive all of the fruits and at least one of the gifts. The gifts are given to believers as God wills so that each church unit might function as Jesus did in the community in which it is placed. Further, the separate gifts were given to each saint so that the members of the church would be interdependent. This was God's means of assuring that the body would not be divided and that no member would be superfluous or proud (1 Corinthians 12:7–27). Then when the church would serve the local community in unity of spirit and purpose, it would reflect the aroma of Christ in grace, peace, and power.

# Intercede for Believers

After empowering, teaching, and gifting believers, the next significant purpose of the Holy Spirit is to intercede personally for each believer. This purpose is outlined in the following verses:

> Likewise the Spirit also helps in our weaknesses. For we do not know what we should pray for as we ought, but the Spirit Himself makes intercession for us with groanings which cannot be uttered. Now He who searches the hearts knows what the mind of the Spirit is, because He makes intercession for the saints according to the will of God.
>
> ROMANS 8:26–27 (NKJV)

Now there are several things to note here. The first is that Christians often do not know how they should pray about an issue. One might have two or more job options or ministry opportunities, for example, and not know which one to take. The road of life has many forks, and choices must be made at each one. And when one way is chosen, frequently there is no option of turning back to choose the other one if circumstances change. So which path should one take? Often one simply doesn't know. In such cases, Christians have an outstanding advantage. The Holy Spirit intercedes for them with "groanings which cannot be uttered." Why does he intercede with such intensity? Because the will of God is at stake in the saint.

Our choices do matter to God. He does have a plan for every believer's life (Ephesians 2:10), and the Holy Spirit is interceding so that we will fulfill it. Hence, when Paul's plan to go to Asia was blocked by the Holy Spirit, God gave him a vision that he should go to Macedonia instead (Acts 16:6–9). The Bible does not explain God's reasons for changing Paul's preferred itinerary. It does clearly state, however, that the Holy Spirit intervened to guide Paul into the will of God in these choices. The Letters to the Philippians, the Thessalonians, and the Corinthians are ample evidence today of the importance of Paul's having followed the Spirit's leading into Macedonia at that time.

Jackie and I had a similar experience when we were planning our first full-time mission. I'd taken several short-term mission trips to Haiti (a couple of them with Jackie), had learned a little Creole, had made several friends and contacts in the country, and had been given a genuine love of the people by the Lord. I'd even seen God work miracles there. I was really pumped up to go and work in that part of God's vineyard. But when the time came for me to do a missions internship for my master of divinity at seminary, the denomination sent me to Baguio City in the Philippines. I had been to Baguio City for an R&R during the Vietnam War, and I knew it was no hardship tour. So I'd gladly accepted, and Jackie and I and our youngest son headed to the Philippines in July 1991 during the peak of the rainy season. We landed there after an 8 on the Richter scale earthquake in 1990 and about two weeks after Mount Pinatubo had blown. Lahar (volcanic ash) and wreckage littered the landscape.

The trip was very challenging in many ways, but spiritually it was awesome. The cat-sized rats in the walls next to our bed at night, the incessant rain, the drastic dietary change, and many other cultural issues worked on both my wife and son. Our skinny, fifteen-year-old son lost sixteen pounds in two months. At the end, we had experienced many spiritual blessings, but we were physically and emotionally drained. None of us expected to return. But in my heart, a new seed had been planted.

When I graduated from seminary and we began to seriously consider our ministry options, I suggested to Jackie that we return to the Philippines at a nicer time of the year and talk to the pastor who invited us to help him in 1991. She agreed. We were cordially welcomed by all, the weather was much nicer, and Baguio seemed much less formidably foreign. But serious reservations continue to plague my wife, so after about ten days, we returned, discouraged with the prospects. I then began a time of intense prayer about God's will for our lives. The Holy Spirit must have also been interceding because, after several weeks, I was given an unmistakable, vivid vision calling me to Asia. That ended the issue for me. I praised God for making his will clear to me on this important decision.

Unfortunately, as many of you married folks may have guessed, it didn't settle the issue for Jackie. After all, God did not show her the vision; and because of her serious reservations about life in the Philippines, she really wanted to hear from God herself. So God, in his mercy and love, confronted her in the shower one morning. He asked her, "Are you one flesh with Rick? [Matthew 19:5–6] If I have called him, I have also called you. Go together." That settled it in my wife's heart, and we went with anticipation to our mission. I'm certain that the Holy Spirit had interceded for us with the Father and that he had granted his request. The next thirteen years in the

Philippines were the most productive, challenging, joyful, and fulfilling of my entire life. And I never would have guessed ahead of time that that would be the case. The safest and best place to be in this world is in the will of God. What a blessing to have God on our side! And what an important Intercessor to have, not only at the vital crossroads but even in the seemingly trivial encounters of our lives. You never know when God is going to bring an important surprise in your life that will require spiritual strength and wisdom.

## Summary

Jesus commanded his handpicked students and executives—a motley crew of fishermen, a zealot, a tax collector, etc.—not to leave Jerusalem until they had received the promise of God (Acts 1:4). That promise was the washing and infilling of the Holy Spirit. Jesus knew that no man, no matter how much knowledge and training he had, could lead a righteous life and impart the beauty and power of the multifaceted gospel of the kingdom of God without being born again and being filled with the Holy Spirit of Jesus Christ. The "old" man without Christ simply cannot touch the love, wisdom, or beauty of the Spirit-empowered, "new" man in Christ. In fact, 1 John 4:9 expressly states that it is God's purpose that born-again Christians live their lives through (Greek *dia*, "through" or "by means of") Jesus Christ, and the Holy Spirit is the agent of this new life and the empowerment to fulfill that purpose.

When a person is immersed in the Holy Spirit, all things become new: new birth (born- again), new heart, new Parent, new citizenship, new mind, new strength, new gifting, new power, and new Intercessor! While it is true that Jesus destroyed the strongholds of Satan, sin, and death and thereby saved mankind from mortal bondage, it was nevertheless the role of the Holy Spirit to take the emancipated believer and transform him or her into a victorious and powerful member of God's kingdom.

Look at Peter: strong, decisive, impulsive, intelligent, leader. He swore to Jesus that he would never deny him, and in his heart and mind I believe he really meant it. But when confronted with being killed himself as an important "coconspirator" of Jesus, he denied that he knew him three times, the last with cursing. Then he wept bitterly (Matthew 26:73–75, KJV). The spirit was willing, but the flesh was weak (Mark 14:38). And that was the problem that Jesus knew and anticipated beforehand. But notice what happened after Peter received the baptism of the Holy Spirit in Acts 2ff. He preached with boldness and was fearless in confronting the very chief priests and leaders who had crucified Jesus.

What was the difference between the "before" and "after" of Peter? What had changed his heart from fear to confidence and boldness? The promise of the Father was the difference. The Holy Spirit within changed and empowered him. He had been born again and given a new heart and a new mind upon which were written the laws of God. He was now more than a conqueror through Jesus Christ who loved him (Romans 8:37).

Now that is an awesome change! And that is precisely the change that is available to every Christian today. The only difference between Peter and us is God's specific purpose for our lives in our circumstances today. All the gifts and callings of the early church are still in God's hands and are distributed by the Spirit, as he wills, to every born-again Christian (1 Corinthians 12:7–11). God's purpose in sending the Holy Spirit continues to be to transform hearts and minds, to conform them to the image of Christ, and to empower them for godly ministry. No amount of knowledge or natural ability or effort can even come close to the personal perfection and effective ministry that God is offering to each member of his body through his Holy Spirit.

# The Purposes of God in Man

That man was special to God is clear from the very beginning. He was his last creation. He was the only creation made in God's own image. He was the only one that God walked with and talked with on a personal level. He was the only one to whom he gave dominion over the fish of the sea, over the fowl of the air, over the cattle, and over all the earth and every creeping thing that creeps upon the earth. He's the only one he told to fill the earth and subdue it (Genesis 1:26–31).

The facts and the purposes referenced above have never changed. What has changed is God's relationship with both Satan and mankind. Satan was the covering cherub who walked and talked with God in heaven and who was perfect in all his ways until iniquity was found in him (Ezekiel 28:12–15). He became proud, and he wanted to be worshipped as God (Isaiah 14:12–14). He was the first of creation to rebel against God and to seek the glory and honor that belong to God alone. But he was not the last. Seeing the vulnerability of man in the garden, Satan came upon Adam and Eve, and with subtlety and deceit, he tempted Eve to sin. And what were the temptations? These are to break God's specific commandment, to deny the penalty for disobedience, and to be as God (Genesis 3:1–5).

I review these facts because the root issue of all sin is, "Who rules in my life, me or God?" and "Whose word is true—God's, Satan's, or man's?" The answers to these questions determine our worldview, our values, our ethics, our thoughts, and our actions.

When Adam and Eve chose self and Satan, they rejected God's authority and truth. They believed the lie and suffered the consequences. They were thrown out of the garden and separated from God. Their progeny ultimately also followed their lead. Relationships became so evil that in Genesis 6 we find the following observations:

> Then the LORD saw that the wickedness of man was great in the earth, and that every intent of the thoughts of his heart was only evil continually. And the LORD was sorry that He had made man on the earth, and He was grieved in His heart. So the LORD said, "I will destroy man whom I have created from the face of the earth, both man and beast, creeping thing and birds of the air, for I am sorry that I have made them." But Noah found grace in the eyes of the LORD.
>
> GENESIS 6:5–8 (NKJV)

> The earth also was corrupt before God, and the earth was filled with violence. So God looked upon the earth, and indeed it was corrupt; for all flesh had corrupted their way on the earth. And God said to Noah, "The end of all flesh has come before Me, for the earth is filled with violence through them; and behold, I will destroy them with the earth."
>
> GENESIS 6:11–13 (NKJV)

These verses are pregnant with information and questions. First, they assert that the wickedness of man was so severe that his thoughts were continually evil. Not only had they rejected God, but they had also engaged in all the types of behavior that engender frustration, anger, bitterness, hatred, and strife in one another. Lust, perversion, and corruption ruled. It had gotten so bad that God was sorry that he had created man, and he determined to destroy him.

This latter fact raises a major problem for all who stress the sovereignty of God over the choices of man. Those who say that God predestines the actions of each and every individual and that man has no choices in his behavior would have to ask themselves why God was angry when the men he predestined to sin did so. Five-point Calvinists say that "God decrees sin" and that "all things, including sin, are brought to pass by God."[1] This would make God the author of evil, beginning with Adam and Eve being tempted through the predestined actions of his created being, Satan. But the Bible says that God is light, and in him there is no darkness (sin, wickedness) at all (1 John 1:5). It also says that he is righteous, holy, and good (Psalm 99:9, 119:137, 100:5). Nowhere does it say or imply that he is evil. In fact, attributing the works of Satan to God is the only unforgivable sin (Mark 3:28–30). In Genesis 6, God is clearly angry with man for his evil thoughts, his sin, and his rebellion. All of these emanated from choices to exalt self over God, and all resulted in judgment.

There was one man, however, who found grace with God: Noah. But why? What made Noah different? Note what the Bible says about him:

> This is the genealogy of Noah. Noah was a just man, perfect in his generations. Noah walked with God.
>
> Genesis 6:9 (NKJV)

> By faith Noah, being divinely warned of things not yet seen, moved with godly fear, prepared an ark for the saving of his household, by which he condemned the world and became heir of the righteousness which is according to faith.
>
> Hebrews 11:7 (NKJV)

> And did not spare the ancient world, but saved Noah, one of eight people, a preacher of righteousness, bringing in the flood on the world of the ungodly.
>
> 2 PETER 2:5 (NKJV)

Noah was a character foil to all who were around him. Whereas they were characterized as wicked and evil, the Bible notes that he was a righteous man, perfect in all his "generations"; and he walked with God. Furthermore, while others probably thought he was a fool, he preached righteousness and feared God. So when God told him to build an ark because he was going to destroy the earth with a flood, he did not balk in unbelief. By faith, he began the century-long undertaking despite the critics around him, and he did exactly what he was told to do (cf. Genesis 6:12, 7:5).

For these character traits, Noah and his family were saved, and he became the archetypical example of what God expects man to be in a fallen world, even without his Holy Spirit. Why do I say that? Because that's what Paul says:

> For the wrath of God is revealed from heaven against all ungodliness and unrighteousness of men, who suppress the truth in unrighteousness, because what may be known of God is manifest in them, for God has shown it to them. For since the creation of the world His invisible attributes are clearly seen, being understood by the things that are made, even His eternal power and Godhead, so that they are without excuse.
>
> ROMANS 1:18–20 (NKJV)

So "I didn't know that!" or "Why didn't someone tell me?" is no excuse. One of the saddest verses in the Scriptures is, "My people are destroyed for lack of knowledge. Because you have rejected knowledge, I also will reject you from being priest for Me; Because you have forgotten the law of your God, I also will forget your children" (Hosea 4:6, NKJV).

Today, many people have forgotten the law of our god. Some ignored it; others were never taught. Our children, neighbors, and nations are paying the consequences.

So what can we do? What does God expect from man, and how can man meet those expectations? First of all, he expects them to have the same godly attitudes displayed by Noah, Abraham, Job, and others who pleased him.

## Godly Attitudes

Man's attitudes toward God and neighbor directly affect his judgment and behavior. His faith, his priorities, his fear, and his obedience all weigh heavily on his daily choices and his ultimate destination in life. The Bible repeatedly demonstrates that those with godly attitudes are the ones who have most positively affected the course of human history and who have reaped the rewards of their Maker.

### Faith

As mentioned in the Romans passage above, anyone who denies God's existence is without excuse when his life comes to nothing at judgment day or before. Truly, without faith it is impossible to please God or be saved. Note the following scriptures:

> But without faith it is impossible to please Him, for he who comes to God must believe that He is, and that He is a rewarder of those who diligently seek Him. By faith Noah, being divinely warned of things not yet seen, moved with godly fear, prepared an ark for the saving of

his household, by which he condemned the world and became heir of the righteousness which is according to faith.

HEBREWS 11:6–7 (NKJV)

For by grace you have been saved through faith, and that not of yourselves; it is the gift of God, not of works, lest anyone should boast.

EPHESIANS 2:8–9 (NKJV)

But what does it say? "The word is near you, in your mouth and in your heart" (that is, the word of faith which we preach): that if you confess with your mouth the Lord Jesus and believe in your heart that God has raised Him from the dead, you will be saved. For with the heart one believes unto righteousness, and with the mouth confession is made unto salvation.

ROMANS 10:8–10 (NKJV)

For God so loved the world that He gave His only begotten Son, that whoever *believes in Him* should not perish but have everlasting life.

JOHN 3:16 (NKJV, ITALICS MINE)

Notice that the first critical issue for man is that he "have faith in" or "believe in" God. The whole of Hebrews 11 deals with the importance of faith. It cites example after example of God's heroes who did mighty works and overcame terrible hardships by faith. Noah built an ark when he was told God was going to flood the earth, but it had never flooded before. Abraham was asked to pick up his family and move, not knowing where he went. By faith, Sarah conceived and delivered a child when she was well past menopause. By faith Joshua obeyed God, and the walls of Jericho fell down. None of these people had the New Testament benefit of the indwelling Jesus Christ and his Holy Spirit, yet they had faith in, obeyed, and heard from God.

Sometimes Christians make the mistake of thinking that

having "faith" in Christ or "believing in" Christ is simply giving mental assent to his existence. For example, we can say, "I believe in Santa Claus." What does that ordinarily mean? Usually it means something like, "I believe that there's a fat old man with a white beard walking around in a red-and-white suit, carrying a big bag of gifts to be delivered to children around the world on December 25." Generally, it means we believe that Santa Claus and the stories about him are true. Well, saying "I believe in Jesus" has a very different meaning. It is not mere mental assent to his existence and the veracity of the Bible.

Even Satan believes that Jesus exists. In Job, we see him walking up to God and challenging him about Job's righteousness (Job 1:6ff.). He knows God personally. In fact, he was once a covering cherub, one of God's chief angels.

> You were in Eden, the garden of God; Every precious stone was your covering: The sardius, topaz, and diamond, Beryl, onyx, and jasper, Sapphire, turquoise, and emerald with gold. The workmanship of your timbrels and pipes Was prepared for you on the day you were created. You were the anointed cherub who covers; I established you; You were on the holy mountain of God; You walked back and forth in the midst of fiery stones. *You were perfect in your ways from the day you were created, Till iniquity was found in you.* By the abundance of your trading You became filled with violence within, And you sinned; Therefore I cast you as a profane thing Out of the mountain of God; And I destroyed you, O covering cherub, From the midst of the fiery stones.
>
> EZEKIEL 28:13–16 (NKJV, ITALICS MINE)

So Satan and his demons, fallen angels, "believe" that God exists. But their "faith" or "belief" in God's existence does not save them! Furthermore, the Greek words translated "believe in" are *pisteuo eis* (*πιστεύω* εἰς[2]). The literal translation of these words is "faiths into." While English does not have a verb "to faith," Greek does. In context, then, it says that whoever "faiths into Jesus"—i.e., "by faith becomes one with Jesus"—shall not perish but have everlasting life. Consider how this unity is expressed in the following verses:

> At that day you will know that I am in My Father, and you in Me, and I in you.
>
> JOHN 14:20 (NKJV)

> That they all may be one, as You, Father, are in Me, and I in You; *that they also may be one in Us*, that the world may believe that You sent Me. And the glory which You gave Me I have given them, that they may be one just as We are one: I in them, and You in Me; *that they may be made perfect in one*, and that the world may know that You have sent Me, and have loved them as You have loved Me.
>
> JOHN 17:21–23 (NKJV, ITALICS MINE)

> I have been crucified with Christ; it is no longer I who live, but Christ lives in me; and the life which I now live in the flesh I live by faith in the Son of God, who loved me and gave Himself for me.
>
> GALATIANS 2:20 (NKJV)

So Satan and his demons not only know that God exists, but they are also certain of it. They were even the first ones to acknowledge who he really was!

> When He had come to the other side, to the country of the Gergesenes, there met Him two demon-possessed men, coming out of the tombs, exceedingly fierce, so that no one could pass that way. And suddenly they cried out, saying, "What have we to do with You, Jesus, You Son of God? Have You come here to torment us before the time?"
>
> MATTHEW 8:28–29 (NKJV)

> Then He went down to Capernaum, a city of Galilee, and was teaching them on the Sabbaths. And they were astonished at His teaching, for His word was with authority. Now in the synagogue there was a man who had a spirit of an unclean demon. And he cried out with a loud voice, saying, "Let us alone! What have we to do with You, Jesus of Nazareth? Did You come to destroy us? I know who You are—the Holy One of God!" But Jesus rebuked him, saying, "Be quiet, and come out of him!" And when the demon had thrown him in their midst, it came out of him and did not hurt him.
>
> LUKE 4:31–35 (NKJV)

Consequently, just acknowledging that he exists or "believing in" him in the sense of giving mental assent to his existence or accepting the stories about him as truth is not saving faith. Saving faith is what James, by the Holy Spirit, describes as that faith that manifests itself as actions reflecting that belief, e.g., obedience to God's commands. He puts it this way:

> Thus also faith by itself, if it does not have works, is dead. But someone will say, "You have faith, and I have works." Show me your faith without your works, and I will show you my faith by my works. You believe that there is one God. You do well. Even the demons believe—and tremble! But do you want to know, O foolish man, that faith without works is dead? Was not Abraham our father justified by works when he offered Isaac his son on the altar? Do you see that faith was working together with his works, and by works faith was made perfect? And the Scripture was fulfilled, which says, "Abraham believed God, and it was accounted to him for righteousness." And he was called the friend of God. *You see then that a man is justified by works, and not by faith only.* Likewise, was not Rahab the harlot also justified by works when she received the messengers and sent them out another way? *For as the body without the spirit is dead, so faith without works is dead also.*
>
> JAMES 2:17–26 (NKJV, ITALICS MINE)

James is not contradicting Paul in Ephesians 2:8–9 or suggesting a works salvation. When Paul says that a man is "saved by grace through faith; and that not of yourselves, it is the gift of God, not of works, lest any man should boast," he is simply saying that salvation cannot be earned by man. It was paid for by the blood of Jesus Christ, and it is his unmerited gift to all who will receive him. But once having received Christ as one's Savior and the Holy Spirit as one's comforter and guide, one is expected to work out what God has already worked in as Paul confirms in his Letter to the Philippians:

> Therefore, my beloved, as you have always obeyed, not as in my presence only, but now much more in my absence, work out your own salvation with fear and trembling; *for it is God who works in you both to will and to do for His good pleasure.*
>
> PHILIPPIANS 2:12–13 (NKJV, ITALICS MINE)

Once a person is saved and baptized in the Holy Spirit, it is God who works in him, both to do good works and to want to do them. We want to accomplish the things that God has before ordained that we should do (Ephesians 2:10). We want to obey his commands. We want to love the Lord our God with all our heart and soul and mind and strength. We want to love our neighbors as ourselves (Mark 12:29–31). In other words, our faith is empowered by God to produce godly attitudes and works. It is Jesus himself who becomes the author and finisher of our faith (Hebrews 12:1–2). This is the genuine Christian faith that produces fruits of righteousness and holiness and that brings the kingdom of God on earth. This is the faith about which James was speaking, a faith that manifests itself in godly works.

Now it is true that there are several types of faith referenced in the Scriptures. The first is the faith that emanates from the prevenient grace of God in creation. This is the faith that enables all mankind to know that God exists simply by reflecting on the wonders, beauty, and complexity of nature (Romans 1:18–20). Nobody can thoughtfully look at the construction of a bird's feather or the intricate complexity of a single living cell and say that these things just happened by chance.

For those whose faith is weakened by the current claims of evolutionists, let me digress here a moment to consider just one of the important scientific factors that preclude evolution. Mathematicians and scientists have calculated the probability of the natural origin of the smallest living entity, considering the specific genetic problem of the racemization of the amino acids, which compose DNA. Given the energetically favored process of racemization, the probability of the evolution of the smallest living cell is a vanishingly small, $1 \times 10^{340,000,000}$.[3] Considering that the estimated total number of atoms in the entire universe is only about $5 \times 10^{78}$,[4] it's obvious that the theory of evolution lies dead at the feet of the chemical process of racemization. No DNA could have possibly evolved from a primordial soup of amino acid enantiomers since, except in rare instances, all amino acids in living things are left-handed. Right-handed enantiomers, which occur in equal numbers with left-handed in natural mixtures, simply do not function chemically in living DNA; and if there is no DNA, then there is no life. Even Nobel laureate and famed chemist Dr. Harold Urey acknowledges the problem: "Well, I have worried about that [racemization] a great deal and it is a very important question … and I don't know the answer to it."[5] God does. He deliberately made the evolution of DNA so mathematically improbable that scientists who discovered the process of racemization would acknowledge that this favored chemical process precludes the possibility of evolution. Life could have only come from life, which is the simplified expression of the biological law of biogenesis.[6] Therefore, any deliberate rejection of the empirical evidence legitimizes his anger with anyone who ignores his existence and his role as Creator of all things. For their willfully unwise choice, he gives them over to vile affections and a reprobate mind (Romans 1:18–32). Those who acknowledge the truth, however, are encouraged to review the increasing volume of scientific evidence for creation and be confirmed in their faith.

A second type of faith noted in the Scriptures is the faith that is imbued within the heart and mind of every believer when he or she hears the gospel and receives Jesus Christ as his or her personal Lord and Savior. This is that form of faith that is authored and finished by Christ (Hebrew 12:2) and that results in salvation and the fulfilling of God's righteous plans in the life of the believer, as described in Ephesians 2:8–10.

A third type of faith, the spiritual gift, is mentioned in 1 Corinthians 12:9 and is given to specific individuals as the Holy Spirit wills. How this spiritual gift is specifically manifested is not delineated in the Bible. I suspect it is the type necessary for people to boldly proclaim the gospel before their enemies, knowing that their teaching may mean their death. It may be the faith necessary for God to display signs and wonders on behalf of the petitioner. It may be the faith necessary for a person to lay down his life for his friends. For some, it may be the faith necessary to live just one more day in the face of their circumstances.

Truly, the first expectation of God for man is that he recognizes him for who he is: the great I Am, the Jehovah God of creation and the Scriptures. For, indeed, without faith, it is impossible to please God. Those who come to him must believe that he exists and that he is a rewarder of those who diligently seek him (Hebrews 11:6). Any degree of faith less than this is tantamount to rebellion or indifference to his existence and power. Why? Because faith is the substance of things hoped for and the evidence of things not seen (Hebrews 11:1). Faith that brings salvation has both substance and evidence by which one's loyalty to, and love of, God is manifest in a person's actions and attitudes.

## Proper Priorities

The second vitally important attitude that God requires from a man is that his priorities reflect that he knows him intimately. God has made man in his own image (Genesis 1:26), given him dominion over his creation (Genesis 1:28), and made him a little lower than the angels (Psalm 8:3–6). Because of all these things, he wants to have a personal relationship with each of his highly equipped "management team"—mankind. He wants to be known and understood by all. He wants them to know his management objectives, his personnel policies, his operations and maintenance plans, his strategies, his tactics, his rewards program, his retirement plan, and his disciplinary actions. But most of all, he wants them to know and love his character and to be totally loyal to him only.

It is not enough that man love research in the sciences or humanities. It is not enough: to look through microscopes and telescopes, to dig through ruins and geological formations, to experiment with rats and fruit flies, to ponder precipitates, to analyze history, to characterize anthropological distinctiveness, to hybridize or fertilize. Man has dabbled at all of these things and more, but he still has not discovered through empirical science alone who God is or what he has done. Although it is staring him in the face through the astounding complexity, interdependence, and harmony in nature and astronomy, he still refuses to believe that somehow chance didn't create these things. He refuses to look at the second law of thermodynamics (*there is a tendency in nature to proceed toward a state of greater molecular* disorder[7]) and understand entropy. Instead of noting the inexorable movement toward disorganization and chaos, he insists that things are spontaneously getting more complex, more harmonious, and more physically adapted. In the face of hundreds of extinctions and no evidence of the evolution of new and more complex species, he has hardened his heart against God. It's not that he can't see; it's that he won't see.

That's why Jesus said, "For judgment I have come into this world, that those who do not see may see, and that those who see may be made blind" (John 9:39, NKJV).

For all of man's emphasis on education and the explosion of knowledge in the last century, we still haven't learned to live together in harmony or to bless the gifts and talents of other people. We still haven't learned to share and to manage for the benefit of all or to love God our Creator or to love man our neighbor. Truly, we are among the most ignorant, rebellious, and bellicose creatures to live on the earth.

Is there an answer to all these problems? Can man live in harmony together? Yes! Our Creator has provided the answer. God's first priority is for man to seek and find him. It is in that relationship, and that relationship only, that man can truly prosper individually, collectively, and creatively. It is in that relationship that he can come to know God and his righteousness. With that knowledge, man can then establish appropriate priorities in life. Consider carefully what the following texts admonish man to do:

> But seek first the kingdom of God and His righteousness, and all these things shall be added to you.
>
> Matthew 6:33 (NKJV)

> So I say to you, ask, and it will be given to you; seek, and you will find; knock, and it will be opened to you. For everyone who asks receives, and he who seeks finds, and to him who knocks it will be opened. If a son asks for bread from any father among you, will he give him a stone? Or if he asks for a fish, will he give him a serpent instead of a fish? Or if he asks for an egg, will he offer him a scorpion? If you then, being evil, know how to give good gifts to your children, how much more will your heavenly Father give the Holy Spirit to those who ask Him!
>
> Luke 11:9–13 (NKJV)

> But from there you will seek the LORD your God, and you will find Him if you seek Him with all your heart and with all your soul.
>
> DEUTERONOMY 4:29 (NKJV)

> And you will seek Me and find Me, when you search for Me with all your heart.
>
> JEREMIAH 29:13 (NKJV)

As one can easily see, seeking and finding God is not automatic. Neither is it a task for the faint of heart. It requires diligence, perseverance, and proper priorities. If we set the goal of finding and knowing God as our first priority, we will find him. If we seek him with all our heart and all our soul, we will be rewarded with discovery. But if we expect our parents, our friends, our pastor, or some evangelist to spoon-feed us all we need to know, we'll never discover the fullness of God for ourselves. Even if we attended church every Sunday of the year, and the pastor preached on five verses every Sunday, we would only have heard 260 verses of scriptures. But the book of Matthew alone has 1,118 power-packed verses! How could anyone know or understand the life of Christ or the full counsel of God by attending church once a week and hearing only 260 verses of the Bible in a year? It's like putting three brushstrokes on a large canvas and saying, "There, now do you understand what God looks like?" And the worst part is that only a few of us care enough to try to fill in the blanks, and most cannot remember a sermon for more than a week!

Here's what God says about this kind of Christian:

> Whom will he teach knowledge? And whom will he make to understand the message? Those just weaned from milk? Those just drawn from the breasts? For precept must be upon precept, precept upon precept, Line upon line, line upon line, Here a little, there a little. For with stammering lips and another tongue He will speak to this people, To

> whom He said, "This is the rest with which You may cause the weary to rest," And, "This is the refreshing"; Yet they would not hear. But the word of the LORD was to them, "Precept upon precept, precept upon precept, Line upon line, line upon line, Here a little, there a little," That they might go and fall backward, and be broken And snared and caught.
>
> ISAIAH 28:9–13 (NKJV)

This is a very dangerous time in our history, and not just physically. The Bible warns about false teachers, false prophets, and even false christs (Matthew 24:24; 1 Timothy 4:1–2; 2 Timothy 4:3–4). It is not a time to be ignorant about God or his word. Satan has come to earth to steal, kill, and to destroy (John 10:10), and that is what he is attempting to do around the world. He is stealing the truth and substituting lies, deception, and deceit. He is killing millions with sin. And he is trying to destroy the church.

That is why the Spirit has repeatedly admonished us to diligently seek God with all our heart and soul. Okay, but how can we do that? One of the best ways is Bible study. In order to know God well, we must study the Word of God daily, not just learn a line or phrase here and there (Isaiah 28:13), but we must also take large chunks of scripture and digest it, looking at it from every angle and tasting every nuance, so that we may discern God's ways and his heart for handling each individual and situation in its historical setting and circumstances. We should study his dealings with the rich and the poor, the powerful and the powerless, the tax collector and the fishermen, the father and the mother, the soldier and the prophet, the adult and the child, the widow and the orphan, the scribe and the fool. We should analyze God's character, his loves, his hates, his sorrows, his joys. We should examine his commands and compare the end results of the ones who obeyed and those who did not. By doing these things, praying for discernment and understanding through the Holy Spirit and testing our observations against the empirical evidence of their lives and ours, we'll come to love and understand Almighty God and the wisdom of his advice to Joshua:

> This Book of the Law shall not depart from your mouth, but you shall meditate in it day and night, that you may observe to do according to all that is written in it. For then you will make your way prosperous, and then you will have good success. Have I not commanded you? Be strong and of good courage; do not be afraid, nor be dismayed, for the LORD your God is with you wherever you go.
>
> Joshua 1:8–9 (NKJV)

By exercising ourselves with the above, we will also see the wisdom of seeking first the kingdom of God and his righteousness. As mentioned in the first section, Jesus himself is the King of kings and Lord of lords (1 Timothy 6:14–16). Therefore we are to seek the rule of Jesus Christ and his righteousness in our lives as our top priority. We are not to define our own righteousness or accept the world's norms as our ethical and moral standards.

How can we tell if we've really found God and know him? The Bible gives the following answers to that question:

> Beloved, let us love one another, for love is of God; and everyone who loves is born of God and *knows* God. He who does not love does not know God, for God is love.
>
> 1 John 4:7–8 (NKJV, italics mine)

> Now by this we know that we know Him, if we keep His commandments. He who says, "I know Him," and does not keep His commandments, is a liar, and the truth is not in him. But whoever keeps His word, truly the love of God is perfected in him. By this we know that we are in Him. He who says he abides in Him ought himself also to walk just as He walked.
>
> 1 John 2:3–6 (NKJV)

He judged the cause of the poor and needy; Then it was well. Was not this knowing Me?" says the LORD.

JEREMIAH 22:16 (NKJV)

From the 1 John 4 passage above, it's important to note that "*he who does not love does not know God.*" Therefore, since love is the core character trait of God, the first litmus test of whether a Christian really knows God is, "Does he or she manifest Christian love in his or her life?" By "Christian love" we are referring to that form of selfless love that places the well-being of others ahead of our own selfish requirements or ambitions. It is others-centered, not self-centered. In the original Greek, it is the word ἀγάπη[8] or Anglicized *agape*. The King James Version renders it *charity*, and in many ways it is closer to the precise semantic nuance than the vague word *love*, which carries so many and varied English meanings.

Love is the sine qua non of Christianity. It is the first fruit of the Holy Spirit listed in Galatians 5:22–23 and as such, it is the possession of every born-again Christian. It is not something that is only manifested by sensitive men or women. On the contrary, it is a principle part of the character of God that is imparted to every Christian at the time of conversion. As pure water flows from a spring, love flows naturally out of each Christian as the Spirit moves him to do his will. (Consider James 3:10–12.) This agape love is so pervasive that it can be seen in the eyes, sensed in the Spirit, and observed in action by other Christians.

Because of its centrality and heavy emphasis in the Scriptures, much more will be said about love later in this chapter. For now, suffice it to say that agape love is so critical a character trait of each Christian that its absence calls into question whether a person really knows God at all.

The second definitive test about whether a person really knows God from the above texts is, "Does he or she keep God's commandments?" John boldly asserts that anyone who does not keep his commandments is a liar, and the truth is not in him.

Now don't be a Philadelphia lawyer here. I know that Jesus is the antecedent of "his" in this passage, not God the Father. Nevertheless, Jesus is God, and God is one. Further, as the word of God, it was he who spoke to Moses and gave him the commandments in the first place. Notice that when Moses asked the name of the person speaking to him out of the burning bush, God replied, "*I am who I am .... This is My name forever.*"

In several places in the Gospel of John, Jesus uses this same appellation for himself. Of special note is this: "Jesus said to them, 'Most assuredly, I say to you, before Abraham was, *I AM*'" (John 8:58, NKJV). Here, he directly claims to be the eternal *I Am* who spoke to Moses. Therefore, it would be difficult to assert that the Decalogue is not among the commandments to which Jesus (John 14:15) and John (1 John 2:4, etc.) are referring. Further, Jesus even emphasizes this coupling in his salvation dialogue with the rich young ruler (Luke 18:18–23).

Some of you, readers, may object to this test on the basis of Paul's statements in Galatians that if we are led by the Spirit, we are not under the law (5:18) or that Christ has redeemed us from the curse of the law ... that we might receive the promise of the Spirit through faith (4:13–14). To answer these objections, one must first understand that Paul was writing to the Galatians because of the Jewish converts in the church who were trying to make the Gentile members circumcise their males because it was a law given to the Jews forever (Genesis 17:9–14). And there were many such struggles between Jewish background believers and the Gentile believers, over which Jewish laws and traditions should remain applicable to the new Christian church. In the end, Jesus replaced the letter of the law and the curses of the Mosaic covenant in favor of the spirit of the law as instilled by the new covenant, in which the Holy Spirit wrote the applicable laws on the hearts of each Christian and caused them to obey the statutes and ordinances of God (Jeremiah 31:31–34; Ezekiel 36:26–27; Hebrew 8–10). (Note especially Jeremiah 31:34 as the fulfilling of this prophesy concerning the new covenant. It also gives yet another test of knowing God.)

On the other hand, Jesus did not come to destroy the law and the prophets by spiritualizing them either, as some today seem to believe. In fact, he specifically rejected that thought when he said the following:

> Do not think that I came to destroy the Law or the Prophets. I did not come to destroy but to fulfill. For assuredly, I say to you, till heaven and earth pass away, one jot or one tittle will by no means pass from the law till all is fulfilled. Whoever therefore breaks one of the least of these commandments, and teaches men so, shall be called least in the kingdom of heaven; but whoever does and teaches them, he shall be called great in the kingdom of heaven. For I say to you, that unless your righteousness exceeds the righteousness of the scribes and Pharisees, you will by no means enter the kingdom of heaven.
>
> MATTHEW 5:17–20 (NKJV)

What all these verses reveal is that keeping the spirit of the commandments is still very much on God's heart, even in this present age. Jesus himself said, "If you love Me, keep My commandments" (John 14:15, NKJV). Paul, by the spirit, also affirmed this in these verses:

> But now we have been delivered from the law, having died to what we were held by, so that we should serve in the newness of the Spirit and not in the oldness of the letter.
>
> ROMANS 7:6 (NKJV)

> Who also made us sufficient as ministers of the new covenant, not of the letter but of the Spirit; for the letter kills, but the Spirit gives life.
>
> 2 CORINTHIANS 3:6 (NKJV)

In considering this issue, what is so frequently lost in the modern church is that the spirit of the law often places greater restrictions on behavior than the letter of the law. Consider Jesus's teachings on the following:

> You have heard that it was said to those of old, "You shall not murder, and whoever murders will be in danger of the judgment." But I say to you that whoever is angry with his brother without a cause shall be in danger of the judgment. And whoever says to his brother, "Raca!" shall be in danger of the council. But whoever says, "You fool!" shall be in danger of hell fire.
>
> Matthew 5:21–22 (NKJV)

> You have heard that it was said to those of old, "You shall not commit adultery." But I say to you that whoever looks at a woman to lust for her has already committed adultery with her in his heart.
>
> Matthew 5:27–28 (NKJV)

> Furthermore it has been said, "Whoever divorces his wife, let him give her a certificate of divorce." But I say to you that whoever divorces his wife for any reason except sexual immorality causes her to commit adultery; and whoever marries a woman who is divorced commits adultery.
>
> Matthew 5:31–32 (NKJV)

The silver lining to all this is that God understands man's weaknesses and the historic failures of his chosen people and has decided to send the Holy Spirit of his Son to live in man, to give him both the power and the attitude necessary to keep his commandments and walk as his Son walked. Consider what Paul says about these truths in Galatians alone:

For you are all sons of God through faith in Christ Jesus. For as many of you as were baptized into Christ have put on Christ.

GALATIANS 3:26–27 (NKJV)

And because you are sons, God has sent forth the Spirit of His Son into your hearts, crying out, "Abba, Father!" Therefore you are no longer a slave but a son, and if a son, then an heir of God through Christ.

GALATIANS 4:6–7 (NKJV)

My little children, for whom I labor in birth again until Christ is formed in you.

GALATIANS 4:19 (NKJV)

If we live in the Spirit, let us also walk in the Spirit.

GALATIANS 5:25 (NKJV)

God really wants the mind of his Son Jesus to be formed in us. Christ never rebelled against his Father. He obeyed his will in everything, even going to a brutal death on the cross. For these same reasons, he places his Spirit into all who ask him for him (Luke 11:13). When he does so, the born-again Christian receives the same power and desire to obey God and keep his commandments that Jesus had. These commandments are written on his heart and his mind. Therefore, keeping the spirit of the commandments is a valid and important test today of whether a person really knows God and is filled with his Spirit.

In summary, then, seeking and knowing God must be our first priorities. But setting these godly priorities is not always easy. Today's families are jam-packed with obligations. Frequently both Dad and Mom have to work to make ends meet. Children have school, sports, and other extracurricular activities. Churches have Sunday schools, prayer meetings, Bible studies, Awana clubs, youth groups, choirs, adult-education options, and various support and civic-action groups. And there are the issues of grandparents and grandchildren. Add to that text messaging, tweeting, e-mailing, playing games and apps, joining a bowling league, a book club, a quilting group, etc. And one can easily blow eighteen hours a day with frenetic activity. All this busyness and these temporal requirements have often left us worn out and burned out at the end of the day. There simply isn't any time to have a quiet time of prayer and Bible study. The tyranny of the urgent keeps us breathless and godless.

It's time to stop our busyness and take stock of what is really important in life. It's time to reevaluate our priorities and establish God's priorities in our lives. It's time to really seek and know God as our first priority. When we do, all other activities will be given their proper precedence, and our giftings will be used for God's glory in his kingdom.

## The Fear of the Lord

Any serious student of the Scriptures cannot fail to be impressed with the number of times that the "fear of the Lord" is referenced as a character trait of utmost importance to prosperity. Sadly, in the modern church the concept is either ignored or watered down to some milquetoast feeling of "awe." One does not readily associate *fear* with the positive *spin*, which pastors and priests are accustomed to attributing to a loving God. We don't often talk about being afraid of God. On the contrary, we assume that we're all friends of God and that he loves us so much that no matter what behavior we manifest, he's grateful that we even acknowledge him and grace the portals of his churches. We generally have a confident and cavalier attitude when entering into his presence, assuming that our dress, rituals, praise and worship teams, and behavior always bring honor to the King of kings. How many of us enter as humble children to hear and obey our Father's will? And why should we? Why should we go to church with a long face?

Actually, beloved, if that last question is yours, you will have missed the point, and you will have missed God's heart with regard to "the fear of the Lord." If you will prayerfully and diligently consider the following verses and their implications on the behavior, wisdom, and prosperity of man, then I believe that the Spirit will quicken your understanding of this important attitude:

> The fear of the LORD is the beginning of knowledge: but fools despise wisdom and instruction.
>
> PROVERBS 1:7 (NKJV)

> The fear of the LORD is the beginning of wisdom: and the knowledge of the holy is understanding.
>
> PROVERBS 9:10 (NKJV)

> The fear of the LORD prolongs days, But the years of the wicked will be shortened.
>
> PROVERBS 10:27 (NKJV)

> The fear of the LORD is a fountain of life, To turn one away from the snares of death.
>
> PROVERBS 14:27 (NKJV)

> By mercy and truth iniquity is purged: and by the fear of the LORD men depart from evil.
>
> PROVERBS 16:6 (NKJV)

> By humility and the fear of the LORD are riches, and honour, and life.
>
> PROVERBS 22:4 (NKJV)

The secret of the LORD is with those who fear Him, And He will show them His covenant.

PSALM 25:14 (NKJV)

Behold, the eye of the LORD is on those who fear Him, On those who hope in His mercy.

PSALM 33:18 (NKJV)

The angel of the LORD encamps all around those who fear Him, And delivers them. Oh, taste and see that the LORD is good; Blessed is the man who trusts in Him! Oh, fear the LORD, you His saints! There is no want to those who fear Him.

PSALM 34:7–9 (NKJV)

As a father pities his children, So the LORD pities those who fear Him. For He knows our frame; He remembers that we are dust .... But the mercy of the LORD is from everlasting to everlasting On those who fear Him, And His righteousness to children's children, To such as keep His covenant, And to those who remember His commandments to do them.

PSALM 103:13–14, 17–18 (NKJV)

Praise the LORD! Blessed *is* the man *who* fears the LORD, *Who* delights greatly in His commandments. His descendants will be mighty on earth; The generation of the upright will be blessed. Wealth and riches *will be* in his house, And his righteousness endures forever.

PSALM 112:1–3 (NKJV, ITALICS MINE)

And I say to you, My friends, do not be afraid of those who kill the body, and after that have no more that they can do. "But I will show you whom you should fear: Fear Him who, after He has killed, has power to cast into hell; yes, I say to you, fear Him!"

LUKE 12:4–5 (NKJV)

> Then the churches throughout all Judea, Galilee, and Samaria had peace and were edified. And walking in the fear of the Lord and in the comfort of the Holy Spirit, they were multiplied.
>
> ACTS 9:31 (NKJV)

> Honor all people. Love the brotherhood. Fear God. Honor the king.
>
> 1 PETER 2:17 (NKJV)

From all the above, it is clear that the "fear of the Lord" is an attitude that emanates from a knowledge and understanding of God and that it imparts many specific blessings. Knowledge, wisdom, riches, honor, eternal life, the secret of the Lord, his covenant, prolonged life, repentance, the eye of the Lord, protection, deliverance, mercy, pity, and provision are all benefits of having a godly fear of the Lord. It is such a foundational concept that it is specifically cited as the beginning of both knowledge and wisdom. Without it, there can be neither.

The founders of Harvard University and many of the other Ivy League schools understood this. Harvard had the following student requirements:

> Let every student be plainly instructed and earnestly pressed to consider well the main end of his life and studies is to know God and Jesus Christ which is eternal life, John 17:3, and therefore to lay Christ in the bottom, as the only foundation of all sound knowledge and learning. And seeing the Lord only giveth wisdom, let everyone seriously set himself by prayer in secret to seek it of Him. Proverbs 2:3 Everyone shall exercise himself in reading the Scriptures twice a day, that he shall be ready to give such an account of his proficiency therein.[9]

In 1746, the first president of Princeton University, Rev. Jonathan Dickinson, declared, "Cursed be all that learning that is contrary to the Cross of Christ!" Until 1902, every president of Princeton after him was a minister. Ditto for Yale University (1701–1898).[10]

Unfortunately, many of these famous institutions have now rejected the fear of the Lord and with it the source of knowledge and wisdom. Consequently, this nation and the world are suffering from a long line of scholars with little or no knowledge of God or the disciplines, which engender harmonious relationships and prosperity. Furthermore, the blessings attendant to the fear of the Lord have been withheld and the specter of 9/11 and its spiritual implications hang heavily over the USA and all other tribes and nations that have rejected him.

While it is true that the fear of the Lord is not highlighted as frequently in the New Testament, it is nevertheless mentioned as an important foundational attitude in the church. Note that all the churches in Judea, Galilee, and Samaria "walked in the fear of the Lord" and that Peter commanded his readers to "fear God." Jesus himself commanded his disciples to "fear Him who, after He has killed, has power to cast into hell; yes, I say to you, fear Him!" This is a clear reference to the white-throne judgment over which he himself will preside! The implications of these teachings are obvious: the "fear of the Lord" is a New Testament attitude that is applicable to the modern church.

Furthermore, one must not soften the impact of this attitude by claiming that *fear* means only *awe* or *reverence*. While both meanings are acceptable for the Hebrew and Greek words translated as *fear*, neither one portrays the concept of knee-knocking terror, which is also in its semantic range. In fact, the Greek verb used in the New Testament passages is *phobeo* (φoβέω[11]), which is the root of the modern English word *phobia*. So if you consider Jesus' command above, awe hardly seems the appropriate emotional response to the possibility of being thrown into hell. Anyone who has meditated on the case of Ananias and Sapphira in Acts 5:1–11 will also be challenged by the severity of the judgment and the subsequent "great fear" that fell on all in the church and upon as many others who subsequently heard these things. The fear mentioned in this context is obviously not just *awe* or *reverence*.

At this point, distinguishing between the godly "fear of the Lord" and the unholy fear of Satan is important. One is the fear of a benevolent, righteous father; the other is the fear of a malevolent, lying killer. While both modify behavior, the motivations of each are qualitatively and quantitatively different. The fear engendered by a benevolent father is that which modifies behavior toward obedience and safety and away from rebellion and danger. It is a type of fear that fills a child who, after being warned, is spanked for running out into the middle of a busy street. The fear of either death or further discipline motivates the child to obey his father the next time and thus remain safely in his play area. Similarly, the fear of the Lord motivates believers to righteousness and freedom from the bondage of sin, wickedness, and death. Perhaps David, by the Spirit, described it best: "The fear of the LORD is clean, enduring forever" (Psalm 19:9, NKJV). There's nothing "dirty," nothing evil, nothing unrighteous, nothing unjust, nothing arbitrary or capricious about the fear of the Lord.

Conversely, satanic fears have quite the opposite effect on people. Anyone who has lived in an animist culture quickly becomes aware of the bondage of people to the fear of satanic spirits. These fears drive the people to make some sort of sacrifice to appease the spirits of the dead, or to chant and dance in order to have some demon possess a member of the group, or to put amulets on various parts of their bodies to ward off many types of evil. Others are in bondage to the orientation of windows and doors in their buildings, curses placed on them through various "colors" of magic (e.g., black, white, yellow, etc.), the fear of an "evil" eye, addictions to various kinds of fortune-telling ( e.g., horoscopes, astrology, Ouija boards, tarot cards, etc.), hallucinatory drugs, witchcraft, or outright Satanism. These types of fear drive people deeper and deeper into lusts (e.g., power, money, perversions, and addictions), predatory fear, protection rackets, sickness, lawlessness, and poverty. These are "dirty" fears. These are fears that drive people into the bondage of evil and sin. This is the type of fear that one has when one must pay protection money so that he or she would not be assaulted or robbed. This is the type of fear that forces you to toe the "party line" or suffer the dire consequences. This is the terror of demonic possession. This is the compulsion to commit suicide, kill, or commit some other antisocial act.

Many Westerners who grow up in rationalist cultures will have trouble understanding or accepting the reality of satanic fear and demonic activities in human societies. We are heavily indoctrinated into pop psychology and the denial of the supernatural. We haughtily presume that these poor, benighted people of the Third World are just ignorant and superstitious. To some extent, of course, that may be true, but let us be careful of our own pride, presuppositions, and vulnerability to the deceptions of the evil one. Jackie and I have been in both Haiti and the Philippines, and we are eyewitnesses of demonization, the issues of voodoo (*kulam* in Filipino), and various tribal oppressions of the evil one. We have even known people who were hearing voices in their mind, telling them to kill themselves, who were instantly healed through prayer in the name of Jesus Christ. We suspect that many who are labeled suicidal or schizophrenic are really spiritually oppressed, not mentally ill in the classical sense.

The bottom line is this: the fear of the Lord is the beginning of wisdom and knowledge. It is a positive attitude that God intends all men to have in order to motivate them to obedience and righteousness. Since it is clean and its motivation is righteousness, it is the antithesis of satanic fear and most nearly resembles the attitude of a child who wants to please his father and fears the father's disapproval or anger should he break his rules. As David points out in the Psalms 103 above, this type of fear elicits the pity and mercy of God.

## Obedience

The final attitude that God purposed in man is a logical result of the first three. After beginning in faith, seeking and prioritizing the kingdom of God and his righteousness, and beginning to acquire knowledge and wisdom through the fear of the Lord, the earnest disciple quickly learns that an attitude of obedience unlocks many wonderful promises of his Father. While the Bible does record some unconditional promises of God—such as not to destroy the world again by water, to make the seed of Abraham a blessing to all mankind, and to establish the throne of David forever—by far the majority of his promises are conditional. If his children will obey his commands and continue to walk in his ways, then he will bless them. If they refuse, he will discipline them.

As mentioned earlier in this book, the most dramatic illustration of this linkage is given by Moses when he revealed the first covenant to Israel. Note again the promises of blessing and the conditions for the blessings as related in Deuteronomy 28:

> Now it shall come to pass, *if you diligently obey the voice of the LORD your God, to observe carefully all His commandments* which I command you today, that the LORD your God will set you high above all nations of the earth. And all these blessings shall come upon you and overtake you, because you obey the voice of the LORD your God: Blessed shall you be in the city, and blessed shall you be in the country. Blessed shall be the fruit of your body, the produce of your ground and the increase of your herds, the increase of your cattle and the offspring of your flocks. Blessed shall be your basket and your kneading bowl. Blessed shall you be when you come in, and blessed shall you be when you go out. The LORD will cause your enemies who rise against you to be defeated before your face; they shall come out against you

> one way and flee before you seven ways. The LORD will command the blessing on you in your storehouses and in all to which you set your hand, and He will bless you in the land which the LORD your God is giving you. The LORD will establish you as a holy people to Himself, just as He has sworn to you, *if you keep the commandments of the LORD your God and walk in His ways.* Then all peoples of the earth shall see that you are called by the name of the LORD, and they shall be afraid of you. And the LORD will grant you plenty of goods, in the fruit of your body, in the increase of your livestock, and in the produce of your ground, in the land of which the LORD swore to your fathers to give you. The LORD will open to you His good treasure, the heavens, to give the rain to your land in its season, and to bless all the work of your hand. You shall lend to many nations, but you shall not borrow. And the LORD will make you the head and not the tail; you shall be above only, and not be beneath, *if you heed the commandments of the LORD your God, which I command you today, and are careful to observe them.* So you shall not turn aside from any of the words which I command you this day, to the right or the left, to go after other gods to serve them.
>
> Deuteronomy 28:1–14 (NKJV, italics mine)

All the beautiful blessings promised above were contingent on yielding to God's commandments and walking in his ways. Three times Moses, by the Spirit, reminds the Israelites of the inextricable linkage of blessings to obedience. To further clarify this point and to warn them of the dire consequences of disobedience, he proceeds to share fifty-four verses of horrendous curses that God will personally bring on Israel if they break the covenant by rebelling against its requirements.

Another significant example of the importance of walking in the will of God through obedience is found in the issue of prayer. Most people believe that when they pray, God is listening to them. Actually, that may not be the case. The Bible lists several hindrances to answered prayer that are directly related to disobedience, including the following:

> But your iniquities have separated you from your God; And your sins have hidden His face from you, So that He will not hear.
>
> ISAIAH 59:2 (NKJV)

> If I regard iniquity in my heart, the Lord will not hear me:
>
> PSALM 66:18 (KJV)

> If My people who are called by My name will humble themselves, and pray and seek My face, and turn from their wicked ways, then I will hear from heaven, and will forgive their sin and heal their land.
>
> 2 CHRONICLES 7:14 (NKJV)

> Because I have called and you refused, I have stretched out my hand and no one regarded, Because you disdained all my counsel, And would have none of my rebuke, I also will laugh at your calamity; I will mock when your terror comes, When your terror comes like a storm, And your destruction comes like a whirlwind, When distress and anguish come upon you. Then they will call on me, but I will not answer; They will seek me diligently, but they will not find me. Because they hated knowledge And did not choose the fear of the LORD, They would have none of my counsel And despised my every rebuke. Therefore they shall eat the fruit of their own way, And be filled to the full with their own fancies. For the turning away of the simple will slay them, And the complacency of fools will destroy them; But whoever listens to me will dwell safely, And will be secure, without fear of evil.
>
> PROVERBS 1:24–33 (NKJV)

> One who turns away his ear from hearing the law, Even his prayer is an abomination.
>
> PROVERBS 28:9 (NKJV)

> Ye ask, and receive not, because ye ask amiss, that ye may consume it upon your lusts.
>
> JAMES 4:3 (KJV)

> Husbands, likewise, dwell with them with understanding, giving honor to the wife, as to the weaker vessel, and as being heirs together of the grace of life, that your prayers may not be hindered. [lit. Greek "cut off"]
>
> 1 PETER 3:7 (NKJV)

> *If you abide in Me, and My words abide in you,* you will ask what you desire, and it shall be done for you.
>
> JOHN 15:7 (NKJV, ITALICS MINE)

Beloved, as you reread and meditate on each of the above, I hope that you will begin to see the importance of obedience. We cannot even begin to talk to God until we have dealt with the issues raised above. Jesus himself felt so strongly about this attitude that he said the following:

> Not everyone who says to Me, "Lord, Lord," shall enter the kingdom of heaven, but he who does the will of My Father in heaven. Many will say to Me in that day, "Lord, Lord, have we not prophesied in Your name, cast out demons in Your name, and done many wonders in Your name?" And then I will declare to them, "I never knew you; depart from Me, you who practice lawlessness!" Therefore whoever hears these sayings of Mine, and does them, I will liken him to a wise man who built his house on the rock: and the rain descended, the floods came, and the winds blew and beat on that house; and it did not fall, for it was founded on the rock. But everyone who hears these sayings of Mine, and does not do them, will be like a foolish man who built his house on the sand: and the rain descended, the floods came, and the winds blew and beat on that house; and it fell. And great was its fall.
>
> MATTHEW 7:21–27 (NKJV)

Each of these verses contains a host of sermon topics and reveals one or more reasons why humbly yielding to the will of God is so vitally important, not only for our own benefit but also for the benefit of others. The problem with rebelling against God, i.e., willful sin, is not just that it angers God and brings deleterious consequences on the perpetrator, but it also severely affects those upon whom the sin is directed. For example, the drunken husband not only destroys his own brain and liver, but his aggressive behavior and subsequent stupor also hurt the wife, children, and the economic circumstances of the whole family. The whole family suffers.

Drunkenness is not just a personal issue, and neither is adultery, fornication, homosexuality, murder, envy, sedition, hatred, lying, covetousness, or any other sin. The fundamental problem with sin is that it is selfish and hurts other people. That is why God hates it and why God's laws are all aimed at defining those issues that harm, distort, or destroy relationships, health, stability, justice, truth, etc., and at punishing those who willfully engage in these hurtful behaviors. None of his laws are arbitrary or capricious; they have all withstood the test of time and culture. Further, they are righteous and just. God cannot be bribed. Neither is he a respecter of persons. Both his mercy and judgment are meted out with an even hand to all tribes and nations of the world.

Because he is the Creator and giver of life to all, he has both the wisdom and the right to rule. He has the absolute right to define *good* and *bad*, *right* and *wrong*, and all ethical modes of human behavior. He has the right to define law and enforce it. We have the right to obey or disobey, to receive blessings or curses. We have the right to praise him for being the good, righteous, and holy God who loves us, surrounds us with beauty, and provides for us, or to reject him and his laws as being too restrictive to our personal aims and goals and to our lusts for power, money, perversions, or personal aggrandizement. In the end, we have the right to go to heaven or the lake of fire. We must choose our ruler: God or self, his laws or our laws. Be careful! Our choice on earth determines our eternal condition.

### Summary

Obedience, like each of the other attitudes referenced above, is a choice. In fact, it is a positive attitude that is predicated upon—and cultivated in the presence of—faith in God (the Truth), understanding, and godly fear. The results of it are holiness, righteousness, and peace. James puts it this way: "Now the fruit of righteousness is sown in peace by those who make peace" (James 3:18, NKJV). Consequently, the ultimate result of the positive attitudes God has purposed for man is a just and sustainable peace for all mankind.

Further, whether we like it or not, it is the *only* way to achieve a just and sustainable peace. Peace is not achievable between societies with antithetical worldviews. And don't make the mistake of saying that peace is the absence of war. It is not. It is the presence of godly attitudes—such as love, forgiveness, humility, benevolence, selflessness, generosity, respect, etc.—and the absence of negative attitudes occasioned by envy, strife, bitterness, anger, unforgiveness, hatred, covetousness, selfishness, etc. Sadly, this genuine peace is not the normal condition of man. But it can be! And this will bring us to the pivotal issue of God's purposes for man: death to self.

## Death to Self

Man has a sinful nature. All of history and every newspaper in the world confirm this fact. So does the Bible, in no uncertain terms!

> The fool has said in his heart, "There is no God." They are corrupt, They have done abominable works, There is none who does good. The

LORD looks down from heaven upon the children of men, To see if there are any who understand, who seek God. They have all turned aside, They have together become corrupt; There is none who does good, No, not one.

Psalm 14:1–3 (NKJV)

For there is not a just man on earth who does good And does not sin.

Ecclesiastes 7:20 (NKJV)

As it is written: "There is none righteous, no, not one; There is none who understands; There is none who seeks after God. They have all turned aside; They have together become unprofitable; There is none who does good, no, not one."

Romans 3:10–12 (NKJV)

For all have sinned and fall short of the glory of God.

Romans 3:23 (NKJV)

## The Problem

This fallen state of man—this ubiquitous depravity, this carnal state of rebellion against God, and indifference to the well-being of others—has been, and continues to be, the source of all interpersonal and international maliciousness. Although man has tried many philosophies, psychologies, governments, religions, laws, and organizations, none has provided a lasting peace and a framework for harmonious, multicultural living. And none can, because none deals with man's fallen nature except the body of Christ. We've tried to deal with unrighteousness by wars, laws, jails, and many other forms of behavior modification. But they are all external stimuli or bondage. None deals with man's carnality except our Creator. In short, it is not possible for one person or group of people to force another person or group to conform to their norms of right and wrong without engendering an enormous amount of ill will. We are too hardheaded, independent, and proud to be pushed around by other people or people groups.

Even the modern Christian church is divided and carnal (1 Corinthians 3:3). There are more than 150 "Christian" denominations in America alone. "I am Catholic." "I am Lutheran." "I am Baptist." "I am Evangelical." "I am Pentecostal." There's much strife and division in the church. How can we say that we are not carnal? How many denominations did Jesus Christ establish? Those of us who are pastors ought to carefully consider the following:

> He that descended is the same also that ascended up far above all heavens, that he might fill all things. And he gave some, apostles; and some, prophets; and some, evangelists; and some, pastors and teachers; For the perfecting of the saints, for the work of the ministry, for the edifying of the body of Christ: Till we all come in the unity of the faith, and of the knowledge of the Son of God, unto a perfect man, unto the measure of the stature of the fullness of Christ.
>
> Ephesians 4:10–13 (KJV)

How long did he give us to minister to his body, the church? Until "we all come in the unity of the faith and of the knowledge of the Son of God." Well, are we there yet? Is that even our goal? If not, are we a house divided against ourselves and the will of God? Jesus had some harsh words about a divided house: "But Jesus knew their thoughts, and said to them: 'Every kingdom divided against itself is brought to desolation, and every city or house divided against itself will not stand'" (Matthew 12:25, NKJV).

Sadly, pride and divisions in the church are only the tip of the iceberg. Sin is almost as rampant in the church as it is outside the church. Abortion, homosexuality, premarital sex, adultery, lying, divorce, hatred, jealousy, strife, drunkenness, etc., are all found in the church. And I'm not just talking about the ones who are recovering from their sin or addiction: I'm talking about those who call themselves Christians and are still actively engaged in sin without remorse or repentance. Further, I'm not being judgmental here; I'm simply stating a problem that is emasculating the church and making it irrelevant to a society that desperately needs her Founder and Foundation, Jesus Christ.

## God's Solution

Is there a solution to this problem? Isn't this the way it's always been? Yes and no. Yes, there is a solution; and no, it has not always been this way.

The solution is sublimely simple: we must all die to self (our "old man" or sinful nature). Is that biblical? Absolutely!

> For whosoever will save his life shall lose it; but whosoever shall lose his life for my sake and the gospel's, the same shall save it.
>
> MARK 8:35 (KJV)

> Knowing this, that *our old man was crucified with Him*, that the body of sin might be done away with, that we should no longer be slaves of sin. *For he who has died has been freed from sin.* Now if we died with Christ, we believe that we shall also live with Him, knowing that Christ, having been raised from the dead, dies no more. Death no longer has dominion over Him. For the death that He died, He died to sin once for all; but the life that He lives, He lives to God. *Likewise you also, reckon yourselves to be dead indeed to sin, but alive to God in Christ Jesus our Lord.* Therefore do not let sin reign in your mortal body, that you should obey it in its lusts. And do not present your members as instruments of unrighteousness to sin, but present yourselves to God as being alive from the dead, and your members as instruments of righteousness to God.
>
> ROMANS 6:6–13 (NKJV, ITALICS MINE)

> But you have not so learned Christ, if indeed you have heard Him and have been taught by Him, as the truth is in Jesus: that you put off, concerning your former conduct, the old man which grows corrupt according to the deceitful lusts, and be renewed in the spirit of your mind, and that you put on the new man which was created according to God, in true righteousness and holiness.
>
> Ephesians 4:20–24 (NKJV)

> Therefore put to death your members which are on the earth: fornication, uncleanness, passion, evil desire, and covetousness, which is idolatry. Because of these things the wrath of God is coming upon the sons of disobedience, in which you yourselves once walked when you lived in them. But now you yourselves are to put off all these: anger, wrath, malice, blasphemy, filthy language out of your mouth. Do not lie to one another, since you have put off the old man with his deeds, and have put on the new man who is renewed in knowledge according to the image of Him who created him, where there is neither Greek nor Jew, circumcised nor uncircumcised, barbarian, Scythian, slave nor free, but Christ is all and in all. Therefore, as the elect of God, holy and beloved, put on tender mercies, kindness, humility, meekness, longsuffering; bearing with one another, and forgiving one another, if anyone has a complaint against another; even as Christ forgave you, so you also must do. But above all these things put on love, which is the bond of perfection.
>
> Colossians 3:5–14 (NKJV)

While it is true that God has done everything to deliver us from the guilt and shame of our past sins, that he has saved us from our enemies and has given us new birth and empowerment for righteousness through the Holy Spirit, there still remains one crucial element for all of these blessings to manifest themselves in human behavior: death to self. Paul says that he "dies daily" (1 Corinthians 15:31). If we refuse to die to ourselves or "put off our old man," we will end up in what I call the Romans 7 conflict: the evil things that we don't want to do, we will do, and the good things that we want to do, we will not do (verses 15–20). The law of God, which we acknowledge to be right, will be overcome by the law of sin in our fleshly nature, which we concede is wrong (verses 21–23). In the end, we will say as Paul did, "Oh wretched man that I am! Who shall deliver me from the body of this death?"(verse 24)

This war between the law of God and the law of sin is at the center of the Christian battle for the heart and soul of every man and woman. Paul says that we wrestle not with flesh and blood, but with principalities, powers, rulers of darkness, and spiritual wickedness in high places (Ephesians 6:12). And this spiritual war continues both with unbelievers and carnal Christians. Our real war is not with other people or nations: it is with the spiritual rulers of other people and nations. It is the issue of what and who motivates and drives the decisions of people and nations.

The case of the carnal Christian is of special import to the church today. As mentioned before, because of the common teaching in the church that once one is saved he's always saved, many people who go to church but live in sin have no fear of God and feel secure in their salvation. In fact, however, they are what the Bible calls "Nicolaitans." This is what Dr. C. I. Scofield says about these people: "The name 'Nicolaitan' according to early church fathers [Ignatius, Irenaeus, Clement of Alexandria, Tertullian, Hipolytus] refers to those who, while professing themselves to be Christians, lived licentiously."[12] These were people who claimed to be Christians but whose behavior was not restrained by God's laws. In other words, they believed that their Christian profession through saying the prayer or baptism gave them "license" to live in God's love and grace regardless of their lawless behavior. This is what Jesus has to say about these people in Revelation:

> To the church in Ephesus He said this: "But this you have, that you hate the deeds of the Nicolaitans, which I also hate."
>
> Revelation 2:6 (NKJV)

> To the church in Pergamum He said this: "Thus you also have those who hold the doctrine of the Nicolaitans, which thing I hate. Repent, or else I will come to you quickly and will fight against them with the sword of My mouth."
>
> Revelation 2:15–16 (NKJV)

Paul, by the Spirit, adds the following:

> What shall we say then? Shall we continue in sin that grace may abound? Certainly not! How shall we who died to sin live any longer in it?
>
> Romans 6:1–2 (NKJV)

> What then? Shall we sin because we are not under law but under grace? Certainly not!
>
> Romans 6:15 (NKJV)

James describes those who are Nicolaitans, or carnal Christians, as double-minded persons who are unstable in all their ways (James 1:8). And the Greek word rendered *double-minded* here is *dipsuchos* (δίψυχος[13]), which literally means "two-spirited."[14] On the one hand, they have the Holy Spirit and desire to keep God's laws and do what is right; on the other hand, the "old man" persuades them to rebel and fulfill their sinful desires. They pray, but they waver in their faith. They're constantly in the Romans 7 conflict with the law of God, warring against the law of sin. The new man and the old man are constantly battling, and, in the Romans 7 condition, the old man wins. That is a big-enough problem, but the more serious one is that they don't see the danger of remaining in that deadly position. They honestly think that this is the normal Christian condition and that Jesus will vouch for them on judgment day. They have no fear of the Lord at all. They may confess their sins, but they don't repent of them. This is an ignorant and dangerous position to be. Those of us who are called to be pastors ought to carefully consider Ezekiel 33:7–16, Jeremiah 6:13–19, Jeremiah 7:3–15, and Hebrews 10:26–31. God will not hold us watchmen harmless for allowing his people to commit abomination with impunity and without warning.

## Summary

Death to self is a mountain that every Christian must climb. It is by far the most critical and difficult decision that any man or woman will have to make and continue to make. Most people like themselves the way they are. They have become accustomed to their personal idiosyncrasies and preferences. While their consciences may tweak them when they do something wrong, they nevertheless comfort themselves with thoughts like, "Well, everybody's doing it," or "At least I'm not as bad as so and so," or "My sin is no worse than ——." Psychologists might even call them well-adjusted and productive people. Sociologists or anthropologists may pass their sins off as cultural adaptations, religious anomalies, or personal preferences. Even many Christians shrug their shoulders and say, "Anyway, nobody's perfect," or "That's just the way he is. We'll just have to accept it," or "We must learn to love one another despite our sinful proclivities." Jesus puts it this way:

> If anyone comes to Me and does not hate his father and mother, wife and children, brothers and sisters, yes, and his own life also, he cannot be My disciple. And whoever does not bear his cross and come after Me cannot be My disciple.
>
> LUKE 14:26–27 (NKJV)

We must die to self-rule and self-imposed standards. As long as Christians continue to accept sin and the old man as man's normal state, there will never be true revival in the church. The kingdom of God is predicated on Christ being King and ruling from within the hearts and minds of every Christian person. Jesus will be both Savior and King, not just Savior. He is not some cosmic, effeminate Santa Claus who doles out his gifts of salvation, prosperity, and love to his poor, benighted, and unrepentant children. He is King of kings and Lord of lords! He is the Ruler, and he expects his subjects to obey his laws. His blessings are conditional. They depend on whether we're willing to abide in him and willingly accept his laws, which are based on his foreknowledge of man's character, propensities, and potential, and on his plans to bless mankind with the keys to loving and harmonious living. Therefore man must choose. Either Christ rules in our hearts or we do.

Don't take this issue lightly! Each person's decision on the matter of dying to self is a real life-and-death decision. Self is a formidable obstacle to victorious, righteous living in Christ. It is, therefore, a key purpose of God that man should deny his old sinful nature and receive his new nature to thrive in this world.

Remember in all this that God has given us the mind of Christ and the power of the Holy Spirit within. We have been crucified with Christ so that the body of sin might be destroyed (Romans 6:6). Therefore, we have the power and the desire within us to die to self. But we have to decide to exercise that power and actually do it.

Perhaps an illustration would help here. When I was in school, in a fraternity, and in the Air Force during the Vietnam War, I had a dirty mouth. I could speak the King's English when circumstances dictated, and I could cuss with the boys when I felt like it. I frequently took the Lord's name in vain and even swore in my wife's and children's presence. I went to church almost every Sunday and didn't sense any real problem with my behavior. Anyway, it was only bad language, and "everybody's" doing it.

Then, at a Christian retreat, the Lord got a hold of me, broke my hard heart, and filled me with his supernatural love. I was born again. I don't remember ever swearing or taking the Lord's name in vain again. It wasn't that I couldn't cuss or blaspheme the Lord; it was that I didn't *want* to. My mind and heart had been changed. And whenever I heard another person cursing or violating that commandment, I was not angry; I was hurt, because that's the way I used to sound.

At that time I didn't understand all the theology or biblical principles that would have explained what had happened to me. All I knew was that I heard with different ears and evaluated things with a different mind. Now I understand that God took away and forgave my besetting sins and filled me with his Spirit. I recoiled at my previous ungodly behavior. I saw that it hurt others and demeaned my Creator. I willingly left it or put it off for the joy of a clean conscience and a heart full of love.

So God will not force us to put off the old man; he will empower us to do so. But each person must choose for himself or herself each day and in each situation. While God has done everything to empower us to live victoriously in him, each of us has to decide whether to accept his terms for this victory and die to self or reject them and live only for self. If we accept them, his kingdom will come on earth as it is in heaven, a condition Christ taught his disciples to pray for and the state each member of the church has been taught to pray for since its inception. If we reject them, the world will continue to move inexorably to Armageddon.

## Reformation, Transformation, and Conformation

God intends to reform, transform, and conform the church. Beloved, remember that the church is the body of Christ and that each Christian is a living cell in that body. As such, we have no right to be cancer cells. Cancer cells are alive and proliferative; they just do not function properly. When they multiply into a tumor, the doctors are called in to remove or chemically neutralize the cells so that the body will not be destroyed. Such was the case with God's surgical extraction of Sodom and Gomorrah. Had they not been removed, their perversion and indolence could have spiritually destroyed the entire area, including Israel (cf. Genesis 19:1–9; Ezekiel 16:49–50; Leviticus 18:5–30).

Why does the church think that it is any different from Sodom and Gomorrah or Israel? Israel was God's chosen nation. Yet when they sinned, God allowed them to suffer defeat in battle, dispersed them to the nations, sent them into captivity, and destroyed the land and all but a remnant of the people in AD 70. If God is the same yesterday, today, and tomorrow, what makes us think that it's acceptable as a church or a nation to do the same things that they did with impunity? Did Jesus really die for our sins so that we could continue to live in them? Certainly not! (Romans 6:1–2)

Sin is the spiritual cancer that is destroying mankind and, yes, even the modern church. God has given mankind the cure, but few have availed of his medicine. Some have taken a dose or two but have never completed the prescribed regimen. Consequently they are still sick. Such is the case with much of the modern church. As long as portions of the church condone behavior that God calls abomination, those portions will be anathema in his eyes. Ironically, the church will also be anathema to other people and religions who laugh at the hypocrisy of our profession. Muslims and atheists are among the first to say that they see no difference in behavior between a believer and a nonbeliever in much of the Christian world today.

All who seek Jesus Christ must be reformed, transformed, and conformed. They must come to him in his way and on his terms. No shortcuts, indulgences, or insurance policies are valid or effective. Simple church attendance will not affect the requisite changes God intends for his disciples. Christianity is not osmosed by couch potatoes, and it is not a spectator sport.

## Reformation

It's time to jump-start the reformation. Martin Luther began the process with his *Ninety-Five Theses* in 1517. Since that time, many others have posted their own declarations of reformation. The result has been a proliferation of Christian denominations, each having their own doctrinal distinctions and stalwart proponents. Perhaps the most significant branches to emerge from this tangled vine were the Pentecostal and charismatic movements of the twentieth century, in which churches, hungry for the signs and wonders of the book of Acts, began to recognize that God had given the Holy Spirit for a purpose and that he was still alive, gifting and empowering the church.

Sadly, however, all these attempts to return to the power and purity of the early church have resulted in more disunity and theological strife than ever. Worse, none has resulted in the strong, united, righteous, and holy church that God established in Christ Jesus. The world is looking with hunger and confusion at a church that may inadvertently fulfill the dire warning of Jesus Christ who said, albeit in a different context, that a house divided against itself cannot stand (Matthew 12:25).

What can be done? The church, which is the body of Jesus Christ, not a denomination, must be reformed from within, not from without. It must be reformed by Christ and in his way. He has given specific instructions for this reformation, beginning with the following:

> Jesus answered and said to him, "Most assuredly, I say to you, unless one is born again, he cannot see the kingdom of God." Nicodemus

> said to Him, "How can a man be born when he is old? Can he enter a second time into his mother's womb and be born?" Jesus answered, "Most assuredly, I say to you, unless one is born of water and the Spirit, he cannot enter the kingdom of God. That which is born of the flesh is flesh, and that which is born of the Spirit is spirit. Do not marvel that I said to you, 'You must be born again.' The wind blows where it wishes, and you hear the sound of it, but cannot tell where it comes from and where it goes. So is everyone who is born of the Spirit."
>
> John 3:3–8 (NKJV)

> Then I will sprinkle clean water on you, and you shall be clean; I will cleanse you from all your filthiness and from all your idols. "I will give you a new heart and put a new spirit within you; I will take the heart of stone out of your flesh and give you a heart of flesh."
>
> Ezekiel 36:25–26 (NKJV)

> Therefore, if anyone is in Christ, he is a new creation; old things have passed away; behold, all things have become new.... For He made Him who knew no sin to be sin for us, that we might become the righteousness of God in Him.
>
> 2 Corinthians 5:17, 21 (NKJV)

Beloved, reformation in the church begins with new birth in Christ Jesus. Every Christian must be born again. Since the Scriptures proclaim that our hearts are desperately wicked through our old-man nature, every Christian must have a new heart and a new Spirit. God is not going to try to fix our hearts or do bypass surgery. He is going to give us a brand-new heart, one that is receptive to his word and loving in its character. He's not going to leave us with a wicked nature; he's going to give us a godly Spirit.

The result of this new birth is that we are a new creation: old things have passed away and *all things* have become new. Our entire worldview is changed. Our whole way of viewing science, nature, life, politics, ethics, relationships, the future, and our reason for existence changes. We look at our world through the lenses of God-colored glasses, not the smudged and tinted glasses of our fleshly experience and teachings. Our actions and demeanor reflect the Holy Spirit who resides within us as our teacher, comforter, and guide. We become filled with love, joy, peace, patience, kindness, goodness, faithfulness, gentleness, and self-control. In short, new birth gives us the potential to be true children of God, reflecting the heart and Spirit of God.

True reformation begins with the heart and the spirit, not the mind. It begins with a genuine love of God and a grateful heart that desires to please and honor him. It begins with a heart eager to observe the great commandments:

> "Teacher, which is the great commandment in the law?" Jesus said to him, "'You shall love the LORD your God with all your heart, with all your soul, and with all your mind.' This is the first and great commandment. And the second is like it: 'You shall love your neighbor as yourself.' On these two commandments hang all the Law and the Prophets."
>
> Matthew 22:36–40 (NKJV)

Why begin here? Because true reformation in the church begins with loving God with all our heart, mind, and soul. When we are born again, we have a personal and powerful true-life experience of God's love and majesty. He is no longer a psychological crutch, a theological hope, the musings of some early Middle Eastern people, or a tool to make people behave well. He becomes real! Our spirits are relieved from the guilt of our past sins as we readily confess and repent of the things that we have done to hurt others and God. We begin to understand the damage that sin has done and is doing in this world. We begin to love God because he indeed has first loved us! (1 John 4:19) We begin to understand the significance of what the Father, the Son, and the Spirit have done and are doing in our lives. And as all of these new realizations come crashing into our conscience, we begin to truly love God for who he is and what he's doing.

Consider this. If I commanded you to love me, would you do it? I doubt it. Most of you don't even know me. The same is true with God. The difference is that he has commanded us to love him. As a practical matter, this will not happen unless we have a personal experience with him and know him. God wants each of us to have this experience, i.e., to be born again. He is not willing that any should perish but that all should come to repentance and the knowledge of the Truth (himself) (1 Timothy 2:4; 2 Peter 3:9; John 14:6). Therefore, being born again is not some esoteric experience of a few. It is the common experience of all true Christians, and it is the beginning of true reformation both in each Christian's life and in the church.

When I was young, I used to hear of rebellious and difficult children who were sent to reform schools. Their exasperated parents realized that they were no longer able to teach or control their children and that the only way that these kids would finally learn how to behave in an acceptable and social manner was in a school designed to modify their behavior and give them new goals and attitudes. Likewise, God has looked at the rebellious people of this earth and determined that we all need to be reformed. We all need to learn how to behave in an acceptable and social manner. Our sins were killing us, and our love was growing cold. His solution was rebirth: a new mind and a new heart. It was and is a brilliant and workable plan. Truly, we all must be born again. We all must be reformed.

## Transformation

Although reformation and transformation begin at the same time and overlap in several areas, they each concern different areas of the body. Reformation deals with the heart and spirit of man, whereas transformation deals with the renewal of his mind and thoughts. The principal verse prescribing transformation is found in Romans 12:

> And do not be conformed to this world, but be transformed by the renewing of your mind, that you may prove what is that good and acceptable and perfect will of God.
>
> ROMANS 12:2 (NKJV)

God has specifically purposed that each person desiring to follow his Son Jesus would have a renewed mind that enables him or her to prove what is the good and acceptable and perfect will of God. He does not want his children wandering about, wondering what God wants them to do or not to do. God does not want his children to constantly be asking, "Why, God?" He wants them to know him personally and to understand by his word and his Spirit why his laws are holy and just and good. And with that understanding, God expects his followers to wholly embrace his way and his truth.

In order to arrive at this understanding of God's perfect will, a person's mind must be totally transformed. This transformation essentially comes in two stages: (1) God's impartation of the mind of Christ and (2) man's absorption of the history, illustrations, lessons, wisdom, doctrines, reproofs, laws, and instructions in righteousness contained in the Bible.

**God's Part**

The first stage of transformation occurs when God imparts the mind of Christ to believers. Since the natural man, an unbeliever or carnal Christian, cannot receive or understand the spiritual things of God, it was necessary that God give him the ability to discern and comprehend these things through gifting him with the Holy

Spirit. Otherwise, he would have eyes that did not see and ears that could not hear, as Jesus frequently said of the crowds who followed him. The principle verses here are the following:

> But the natural man does not receive the things of the Spirit of God, for they are foolishness to him; nor can he know them, because they are spiritually discerned. But he who is spiritual judges all things, yet he himself is rightly judged by no one. For "who has known the mind of the LORD that he may instruct Him?" *But we have the mind of Christ.*
>
> 1 Corinthians 2:14–16 (NKJV, italics mine)

> Let this mind be in you which was also in Christ Jesus.
>
> Philippians 2:5 (NKJV)

Beloved, Christianity is a "mystery" religion. Transformation begins with the spiritual understanding of this mystery, that Christ is in us and that we have his mind. To the unbeliever and to those who've not been born again, the concept of a man believing in—and giving his life for—an unseen God is an inconceivable mystery. This mystery, however, has been openly revealed in the following scriptures:

> I now rejoice in my sufferings for you, and fill up in my flesh what is lacking in the afflictions of Christ, for the sake of His body, which is the church, of which I became a minister according to the stewardship from God which was given to me for you, to fulfill the word of God, the mystery which has been hidden from ages and from generations, but now has been revealed to His saints. To them God willed to make known what are the riches of the glory of this mystery among the Gentiles: which is Christ in you, the hope of glory. Him we preach, warning every man and teaching every man in all wisdom, that we may present every man perfect in Christ Jesus. To this end I also labor, striving according to His working which works in me mightily.
>
> Colossians 1:24–29 (NKJV)

For this reason I, Paul, the prisoner of Christ Jesus for you Gentiles—if indeed you have heard of the dispensation of the grace of God which was given to me for you, how that by revelation He made known to me the mystery (as I have briefly written already, by which, when you read, you may understand my knowledge in the mystery of Christ), which in other ages was not made known to the sons of men, as it has now been revealed by the Spirit to His holy apostles and prophets: that the Gentiles should be fellow heirs, of the same body, and partakers of His promise in Christ through the gospel.

EPHESIANS 3:1–6 (NKJV)

Or do you not know that your body is the temple of the Holy Spirit who is in you, whom you have from God, and you are not your own? For you were bought at a price; therefore glorify God in your body and in your spirit, which are God's.

1 CORINTHIANS 6:19–20 (NKJV)

For it is God who works in you both to will and to do for His good pleasure.

PHILIPPIANS 2:13 (NKJV)

So then, those who are in the flesh cannot please God. But you are not in the flesh but in the Spirit, if indeed the Spirit of God dwells in you. Now if anyone does not have the Spirit of Christ, he is not His. And if Christ is in you, the body is dead because of sin, but the Spirit is life because of righteousness.

ROMANS 8:8–10 (NKJV)

The gist of all the above is that all born-again Christians have received the Spirit of Christ in them and have begun to operate in the will of God through the motivation and understanding of the Holy Spirit. Further, all of God's wonderful promises in the Scriptures are fulfilled "in Christ Jesus," and all who are "in Christ Jesus"—his body, the church—are recipients of these promises

(2 Corinthians 1:18–22, esp. 20). That is why everyone ought to underline each time they find "in Christ," "in Jesus," "in Whom," "in the Beloved," "in Him," and "in the Son" in the Scriptures. Read the context carefully and find out what it is that we have or that we do "in Him." The following is just a very short list of some things 2 Timothy and Ephesians 1 alone say that we have, or have been given, "in Christ Jesus":

> Who has saved us and called us with a holy calling, not according to our works, but according to His own purpose and grace which was given to us in Christ Jesus before time began.
>
> 2 Timothy 1:9 (NKJV)

> Hold fast the pattern of sound words which you have heard from me, in faith and love which are in Christ Jesus.
>
> 2 Timothy 1:13 (NKJV)

> You therefore, my son, be strong in the grace that is in Christ Jesus.
>
> 2 Timothy 2:1 (NKJV)

> Therefore I endure all things for the sake of the elect, that they also may obtain the salvation which is in Christ Jesus with eternal glory.
>
> 2 Timothy 2:10 (NKJV)

> And that from childhood you have known the Holy Scriptures, which are able to make you wise for salvation through faith which is in Christ Jesus.
>
> 2 Timothy 3:15 (NKJV)

> Yes, and all who desire to live godly in Christ Jesus will suffer persecution.
>
> 2 Timothy 3:12 (NKJV)

> Paul, an apostle of Jesus Christ by the will of God, To the saints who are in Ephesus, and faithful *in Christ Jesus*: Grace to you and peace from God our Father and the Lord Jesus Christ. Blessed be the God and Father of our Lord Jesus Christ, who has blessed us with every spiritual blessing in the heavenly places *in Christ*, just as He chose us *in Him* before the foundation of the world, that we should be holy and without blame before Him in love, having predestined us to adoption as sons by Jesus Christ to Himself, according to the good pleasure of His will, to the praise of the glory of His grace, by which He has made us accepted *in the Beloved. In Him* we have redemption through His blood, the forgiveness of sins, according to the riches of His grace which He made to abound toward us in all wisdom and prudence, having made known to us the mystery of His will, according to His good pleasure which He purposed *in Himself*, that in the dispensation of the fullness of the times He might gather together in one all things *in Christ*, both which are in heaven and which are on earth—*in Him. In Him* also we have obtained an inheritance, being predestined according to the purpose of Him who works all things according to the counsel of His will, that we who first trusted *in Christ* should be to the praise of His glory. *In Him* you also trusted, after you heard the word of truth, the gospel of your salvation; *in whom* also, having believed, you were sealed with the Holy Spirit of promise.
>
> EPHESIANS 1:1–13 (NKJV, ITALICS MINE)

Consider the great blessings that we have in Christ just from the verses above:

- Salvation
- Holy calling
- Purpose
- Grace
- Faith
- Love
- Persecution (c.f. Matthew 5:10–12)

- Sainthood
- Every spiritual blessing
- Election
- Acceptance
- Redemption
- Forgiveness
- Knowledge of the mystery of his will
- Unity
- Inheritance
- The seal of the Holy Spirit of promise

Not a bad list for only four chapters in the New Testament! All of these and more are gifted to each born-again Christian through the indwelling Spirit of Christ imparted by God. The reception and understanding of these gifts constitutes the first step in the transformation of men's minds. It is one of the key gifts that God has given to man in his purpose to enable him to walk in perfect righteousness on earth.

**Man's Part**

The second part of the transformation of one's mind, however, is man's responsibility. God has given man, through the regeneration/reformation process and the gifting of the mind of Christ, all the framework that he needs to establish a godly worldview. It is now his responsibility to flesh that out through diligent study and application of the word. The eyes of his understanding have been opened, and now it is time for him to fill his mind with godly wisdom. Consider carefully the following admonitions:

> This Book of the Law shall not depart from your mouth, but you shall meditate in it day and night, that you may observe to do according to all that is written in it. For then you will make your way prosperous, and then you will have good success. Have I not commanded you? Be

strong and of good courage; do not be afraid, nor be dismayed, for the LORD your God is with you wherever you go.

JOSHUA 1:8–9 (NKJV)

All scripture is given by inspiration of God, and is profitable for doctrine, for reproof, for correction, for instruction in righteousness: That the man of God may be perfect, thoroughly furnished unto all good works.

2 TIMOTHY 3:16–17 (KJV)

Blessed is the man Who walks not in the counsel of the ungodly, Nor stands in the path of sinners, Nor sits in the seat of the scornful; But his delight is in the law of the LORD, And in His law he meditates day and night. He shall be like a tree Planted by the rivers of water, That brings forth its fruit in its season, Whose leaf also shall not wither; And whatever he does shall prosper.

PSALM 1:1–3 (NKJV)

But he who looks into the perfect law of liberty and continues in it, and is not a forgetful hearer but a doer of the work, this one will be blessed in what he does.

JAMES 1:25 (NKJV)

Finally, brethren, whatever things are true, whatever things are noble, whatever things are just, whatever things are pure, whatever things are lovely, whatever things are of good report, if there is any virtue and if there is anything praiseworthy—meditate on these things. The things which you learned and received and heard and saw in me, these do, and the God of peace will be with you.

PHILIPPIANS 4:8–9 (NKJV)

Study to show thyself approved unto God, a workman that needeth not to be ashamed, rightly dividing the word of truth.

2 TIMOTHY 2:15 (KJV)

> The law of the LORD is perfect, converting the soul; The testimony of the LORD is sure, making wise the simple; The statutes of the LORD are right, rejoicing the heart; The commandment of the LORD is pure, enlightening the eyes; The fear of the LORD is clean, enduring forever; The judgments of the LORD are true and righteous altogether. More to be desired are they than gold, Yea, than much fine gold; Sweeter also than honey and the honeycomb.
>
> Psalm 19:7–10 (NKJV)

Add to these the beautiful acrostic Psalm 119, and the reader will become well aware of the virtues of studying the Word of God. There is no deeper, wiser, or more righteous literature anywhere in the world. No book in the world has sold more copies than the Bible, and no book of antiquity records a more accurate history of early mankind than is recorded in the Bible. No historical person, place, or event recorded in the Bible has ever been disproved to have existed or occurred, and much of it has been substantiated through independent, ancient Near Eastern studies and archaeological discoveries. Its wisdom books are unsurpassed in literature today. Its laws form the foundation of jurisprudence in many nations, including the United States.

But beyond the secular, the study of the ways in which God deals with man in a whole host of historical and ethical situations sheds light on his character and his will. It is through the study and application of the Word that one comes to know God in a far deeper and more personal way. This in-depth knowledge obtained through study, meditation and experience, when filtered through and tempered by the Holy Spirit, then becomes our wisdom and the plumb line against which one measures theological orthodoxy and righteousness.

Transformation, therefore, is not an option for a Christian. We must have the mind of Christ, since he is our wisdom and our righteousness (1 Corinthians 1:30). Humanity has tried for thousands of years to set up self as the ruler of this world. He has tried socialism, communism, capitalism, monarchies, oligarchies, and dictatorships. He has served pantheons, idols, shamans, charlatans, astrology, cults, and occults. He's been enslaved by money, power, sex, drugs, demons, and fear. He has claimed atheism and agnosticism. He has worshipped wood, stone, metals, and synthetics. Where has it all gotten him? Can anyone truly say that we are better off today in terms of man's ability to live peacefully and in harmony with other men? The only way possible to attain this goal is unity of heart and mind in Christ Jesus. Why? One, because Jesus is *the Truth*. Two, because Christianity is the only religion whose God offers his own mind and heart to believers in order to empower them with his wisdom and righteousness. This is anthropologically unique to those in the kingdom of God. It is the antithesis of the satanic control of people groups and nations through demonic possession, deception, hatred, self-actualization, brute power, etc. But to engage and walk in this unique kingdom of God requires the conversion trinity of reformation, transformation, and finally, conformation.

## Conformation

The third essential element of Christian conversion is conformation. The first two elements of reformation and transformation deal with internal changes in man's heart, mind, and spirit. These changes involve one's worldview and motivation. Conformation, however, is essentially behavioral in character. It deals with how one manages life in an environment that is at best neutral and at worst hostile to his worldview. Jesus was crucified, Paul was stoned and beheaded, Peter was crucified, and all of Jesus's original disciples except John were killed for bringing the Good News to those who did not think that their news was particularly good! Christians and missionaries around the world have been killed for sharing their love of the Lord and the gospel of Jesus Christ.

But Christians should not be surprised at this or try to shun it. Righteousness always evokes contempt from those who live in sin or approve of it. Paul reminds us of this when he writes, "Yes, and all who desire to live godly in Christ Jesus will suffer persecution" (2 Timothy 3:12, NKJV). Suffering, therefore, is a natural consequence of living a godly life in an ungodly world. Jesus suffered, and no servant is above his Master (Matthew 10:24). Furthermore, if we suffer, blessed are we! We are to rejoice, for great is our reward in heaven! (Matthew 5:10–12) Paul, therefore, sets forth the earnest Christian desire to be conformed to the resurrection life and the sufferings of our Lord, not because we are masochists, but because we want to be like Jesus and bring the gospel of the kingdom of God to all on earth regardless of the persecutions or dangers involved.

Some verses that describe and qualify this concept of conformation are the following:

> That I may know Him and the power of His resurrection, and the fellowship of His sufferings, being conformed to His death.
>
> Philippians 3:10 (NKJV)

> Who will transform our lowly body that it may be conformed to His glorious body, according to the working by which He is able even to subdue all things to Himself.
>
> Philippians 3:21 (NKJV)

> For whom He foreknew, He also predestined to be conformed to the image of His Son, that He might be the firstborn among many brethren.
>
> Romans 8:29 (NKJV)

The word *conform* here is the Greek verb *summorphoo* (συμμορφόω) or its adjectival cognate *summorphos*[15] (συμμορφός), which literally means "to morph with" or "to render like, to make of like form, or have the same form." God's clear purpose for conformation, then, is to make each Christian into the likeness of Christ. As you can see from the above, every use of the word in the New Testament—and there are only three—deals with some aspect of this work. Its use in verse 10 above has to do with our experiencing death to self (Romans 6:6–7) and a resurrection into the kingdom of God. In Colossians 1:13, Paul calls this process a "translation" (KJV), literally a transfer from the kingdom of darkness to the kingdom of God without the experience of physical death (cf. Ephesians 2:4–7).

But, beloved, take heart! Be strong! Born-again Christians all have the full assurance of hope that our mortal bodies will eventually be conformed to the image of Christ's immortal body. This is what Paul says about this mystery:

> But someone will say, "How are the dead raised up? And with what body do they come?" Foolish one, what you sow is not made alive unless it dies. And what you sow, you do not sow that body that shall be, but mere grain—perhaps wheat or some other grain. But God gives it a body as He pleases, and to each seed its own body. All flesh is not the same flesh, but there is one kind of flesh of men, another flesh of animals, another of fish, and another of birds. There are also celestial bodies and terrestrial bodies; but the glory of the celestial is one, and the glory of the terrestrial is another. There is one glory of the sun, another glory of the moon, and another glory of the stars; for one star differs from another star in glory. So also is the resurrection of the dead. The body is sown in corruption, it is raised in incorruption. It is sown in dishonor, it is raised in glory. It is sown in weakness, it is raised in power. It is sown a natural body, it is raised a spiritual body. There is a natural body, and there is a spiritual body. And so it is written, "The first man Adam became a living being." The last Adam became

> a life-giving spirit. However, the spiritual is not first, but the natural, and afterward the spiritual. The first man was of the earth, made of dust; the second Man is the Lord from heaven. As was the man of dust, so also are those who are made of dust; and as is the heavenly Man, so also are those who are heavenly. And as we have borne the image of the man of dust, *we shall also bear the image of the heavenly Man*. Now this I say, brethren, that flesh and blood cannot inherit the kingdom of God; nor does corruption inherit incorruption. Behold, I tell you a mystery: We shall not all sleep, but we shall all be changed – in a moment, in the twinkling of an eye, at the last trumpet. For the trumpet will sound, and the dead will be raised incorruptible, and we shall be changed. For this corruptible must put on incorruption, and this mortal must put on immortality. So when this corruptible has put on incorruption, and this mortal has put on immortality, then shall be brought to pass the saying that is written: "Death is swallowed up in victory." "O Death, where is your sting? O Hades, where is your victory?" The sting of death is sin, and the strength of sin is the law. But thanks be to God, who gives us the victory through our Lord Jesus Christ.
>
> 1 CORINTHIANS 15:35–57 (NKJV)

Because of this wonderful hope and promise, no Christian need fear, resist, or resent persecution. It goes with the territory. It proves our mettle. When you squeeze a grape, you will quickly know what is inside, sweet or sour! The same is true of Christians.

Returning now a moment to the previous scriptures above, note that while the first two Philippians references are personally and eschatologically important, the third verse from Romans on conformation is by far the most telling with regard to the issue of human perfection here on earth. Paul, by the Spirit, is stating that all born-again Christians are predestined to be molded into the likeness of Christ in this world. Think about that statement! As adopted children of God, our attitudes and actions are to reflect those of Jesus Christ with our family members, our workmates, and with our local, national, and international neighbors. That is our predestined privilege and obligation! It is an awesome calling. Think what the world would be like if all Christians truly understood this, personally owned it, and steadfastly submitted to God's predestined reshaping of our lives into the image of his Son.

God is the Potter and we are the clay (Isaiah 64:8). Some clay is readily moldable; others are hard and dry or watery and weak or slippery and slimy. Therefore, the conformation process of God is tailored to the "consistency" of each of his elect. The beauty of his work, however, is that no matter how big or how small, how powerful or how weak, how educated or how underprivileged, how poor or how rich, how pigmented or how pale, God personally gifts and forms each of us into a vessel useful and valuable in his kingdom (1 Corinthians 12:7–27).

Regardless of the place or position to which God assigns us in his body, each of us has the responsibility to reflect his character and love, to let his light in us so shine before men that they may see our good works and glorify our Father in heaven (Matthew 5:16). We must shine as beacons on a hill to the darkened world in the valley. This is the joyful privilege and result of being conformed to the image of Jesus Christ.

## Summary

Man is God's favorite creation on earth. He is the only one that he made in his own image. He's the only one with whom he walked and talked personally in the garden. He's the only one to whom he entrusted dominion over all other creatures and plants. He's the only one whom he loved so much that he sent his only begotten Son to redeem and save him from the hands of all that hate him.

No such mercy is recorded for the original rebel, Satan, or the other angels that followed him into perdition. Why? Perhaps it was because they had personally seen and spoken with the Father in heaven. They had experienced his love, his glories, his power, and his wonders, and still rebelled and wanted their own selfish power and glory. Satan wanted to be worshipped just as God in heaven (Isaiah 14:12–15). He destroyed the unity in heaven and actually incited war against God (Revelation 12:7–9). When defeated, he was cast out of heaven into the earth, and he brought his divisive and rebellious campaign with him. For these sins there was neither mercy nor forgiveness.

For man, however, God has had compassion. He knew that he had been deceived by Satan, slain by sin, and placed in bondage by the vicissitudes of life, lusts, addictions, and death. He purposed, therefore, to redeem, release, regenerate, and repatriate all who would willingly acknowledge their fallen state, repent of their hurtful and ungodly behaviors, and seek his face in truth with all sincerity.

God took the first steps for man. He sent his Son and his Spirit to prepare, empower, and enable his way.

The second step depended on the soil upon which these wonderful provisions of God landed. The Parable of the Sower clearly describes the various soils and the results of the seeds sown upon them (Matthew 13:3–23). Therefore, if the recipient had "eyes to see and ears to hear," he or she then began to develop the four godly attitudes necessary for regeneration: faith, godly priorities, the fear of the Lord, and obedience or meekness.

The third step is a corollary consequence of the second: death to self. It is here that man puts off the old baggage—the old man, or the old and sinful nature—and replaces it with the new man, the new nature, the mind of Christ. The final step, although itself a corollary of the first three and a progression involving God's personal and individually specific touches and sequences, involves reformation, conformation, and transformation.

When God has taken each individual through this embryonic

development, the result is that the person is spiritually born again. His old worldview has entirely changed. The old has passed away, and all things have become new. He has a new spiritual, but very real, Father. He has new citizenship; he's now a citizen of the kingdom of God and a pilgrim here on earth. He has a new Ruler, Jesus Christ. He has a new heritage; he's a child of God. He has a new and eternal future. He has a new purpose in life: to do the works that God has "before ordained" that he should walk in (Ephesians 2:10, KJV). He has new promises from an Almighty Father who always keeps his word. He has a new intimacy and love that make this new life a joy and a blessing to live. He has a new foundation and strength that come from wisdom and understanding. He has a new appreciation of others and God's creation. He has a new compassion and warmth that transcend national, ethnic, and cultural barriers. In short, he has the life that God intended all men to have since the six days of creation, when he pronounced all things were very good.

# Perfection: The Abandoned Key

Where do all these purposes take us? Why have we taken this arduous road through God's purposes in Jesus Christ, his purposes in the Holy Spirit, and his purposes in man? We've done it to confront one of the greatest deceptions that Satan has placed before man: "Nobody's perfect." While it is true that all have sinned and fallen short of the glory of God (Romans 3:23), that there is none righteous, no not one (Romans 3:10), and that if we say that we have not sinned or that we do not have sin we deceive ourselves and make God a liar (1 John 1:8–10), all of these together compose only half of the whole truth. If they are used to make one believe something that is not true, they become deceptions.

## The Great Deception

All deceptions and lies are fathered by Satan (John 8:44). He is the master of deception. Several times in Scripture, Satan has used God's word to deceive people. In the garden, he told Eve that God did not want her to eat from the tree of the knowledge of good and evil because he did not want their eyes to be opened to know good and evil (Genesis 3:5). This part was true (Genesis 3:7, 22–24). But with this truth, he mixed a lie: "You shall not surely die." Eve was deceived, disobeyed God, and instead of eternally living a pure and loving life in the garden of Eden with God, she was separated from God and the garden, and without the tree of life, she died.

Similarly, when Satan was tempting Jesus, he quoted scripture to him to tempt him to disobey God. Note the following dialogue:

> Then the devil took Him up into the holy city, set Him on the pinnacle of the temple, and said to Him, "If You are the Son of God, throw Yourself down. For it is written: 'He shall give His angels charge over you,' and, 'In their hands they shall bear you up, Lest you dash your foot against a stone.'" Jesus said to him, "It is written again, 'You shall not tempt the LORD your God.'"
>
> MATTHEW 4:5–7 (NKJV)

Satan began with a deception: if you really are the Son of God, jump off the roof! Prove that you are. Then he tried to justify his suggestion by quoting scripture "For it is written: 'He shall give His angels charge over you,' and, 'in their hands they shall bear you up, lest you dash your foot against a stone.'" C'mon, Jesus, prove that you are the Son of God. But Jesus, seeing through the deceit of the devil, countered with another scripture that trumped the devil's and spoke to the truth and heart of the issue: don't put God to the test. Don't do something foolish just to "make" God do something for you.

Satan has tried to deceive mankind in the same way with regard to perfection. He starts with a statement like, "Nobody's perfect." He then quotes several verses of scripture proving that man has fallen into sin, that all have sinned, that all have a sinful nature, and that no one is righteous, not even one. And while these accusations are true of all of us as the natural man who cannot receive the things of the Spirit, they are not true of the born-again Christian in Christ who has put off the old man and put on Christ as Paul describes in his letters and as has been discussed earlier.

So let's praise God for setting us free from the evil one's deceptions and empowering us through his Son and Holy Spirit to have victory in this horrible and tragic battle over sin in the flesh. We're no longer the wretched man in bondage to sin in the flesh. God's Spirit in us has empowered us to walk in righteousness (cf. 1 John 3:4–10 and Ezekiel 36:26–27).

The great purpose of the Scriptures, therefore, is to reveal this great emancipation and God's awesome love, righteousness, power, beauty, character, and purposes. Ever since the fall, God has worked diligently and strategically to bring his favorite earthly creation, man, back into the personal love relationship that he had with Adam and Eve in the garden. First, he isolated Noah, a preacher of righteousness, with his family and cargo of creatures, and then destroyed all life that had breath in order to remove the ubiquitous evil that permeated all of man's thoughts and actions. He determined to start over again. Man's sin so grieved his heart that he regretted that he had even made man (Genesis 6:5–6). When sin shortly reentered the world, he chose Abraham, a man who believed God and whose faith and obedience were counted unto him for righteousness. From him descended a nation of Hebrews to whom were given his covenants and commandments so that their resultant prosperity and righteous laws would be a light to the world and draw all men to God. Then, despite their unique blessings, Israel abandoned the truth and went after the deceptive idols and lusts of the nations around them. Finally, in this battle for the hearts and minds of every man, woman, and child in the world, God pulled out his double-edged sword and sent his Son, Jesus the Christ, and his Holy Spirit into the world to set the people free from the bondage of deception and lies. Jesus is the Truth, and the Holy Spirit is the Spirit of truth. When the smoke of the ensuing battle had cleared, God stood victorious. The Knight had slain the dragon. As was noted earlier, Satan, sin, and death had been destroyed.

## The Abandoned Key

With the bloody battle decided, the soft winds of faith, hope, and love blew off the dust that had covered a beautiful golden key called *perfection*. What had been hidden for centuries with the debris of sin, wickedness, and iniquity was now exposed to man. Since he had never seen the key before, he was at once attracted to its beauty but repelled by its strangeness. And since his own nature doubted its reality and since his mind felt it was a mirage, most men looked at it curiously and walked away.

Jesus asked his disciples, "Who do men say that I, the Son of Man, am?" Consider carefully his answer:

> So they said, "Some say John the Baptist, some Elijah, and others Jeremiah or one of the prophets." He said to them, "But who do you say that I am?" Simon Peter answered and said, "You are the Christ, the Son of the living God." Jesus answered and said to him, "Blessed are you, Simon Bar-Jonah, for flesh and blood has not revealed this to you, but My Father who is in heaven. And I also say to you that you are Peter, and on this rock I will build My church, and the gates of Hades shall not prevail against it. And I will give you the keys of the kingdom of heaven, and whatever you bind on earth will be bound in heaven, and whatever you loose on earth will be loosed in heaven."
>
> Matthew 16:14–19 (NKJV)

God had revealed to Peter the first key to the kingdom of heaven: Jesus is the Christ, the Son of the living God. It was upon this confession, this rock, this foundational truth, that the church would be built. Note that this key was not revealed by man, but by

God. Despite all of Jesus's teaching, compassion, and miracles, the Jews and the Romans were still guessing about who he was. The Romans and the Jewish leaders never did find out. In fact, only his disciples knew. After Pentecost, they became bold enough to proclaim the truth, even though many still could not or would not believe.

Observe also that there is more than one key to the kingdom of heaven. Jesus said that he would give Peter the "keys." His identification of Jesus as the Messiah, the Christ of God, was the foundational key, but it was not the only key. The fundamental doctrinal teachings of the Scripture reveal several other keys. But I believe that because of man's sinful nature, one of the most beautiful keys was abandoned: *perfection*.

Why do I believe that this is a key to the kingdom? Because the scriptures reveal that without holiness, no man shall see God (Hebrew 12:14) and because Jesus commanded us to be perfect (Matthew 5:48).

## Passages Proclaiming Perfection

There are many passages calling on born-again Christians to be perfect and passages even in the Old Testament declaring that certain individuals were perfect or were called to be so. Consider the following examples:

> These are the generations of Noah: Noah was a just man and perfect in his generations, and Noah walked with God.
>
> GENESIS 6:9 (KJV)

And when Abram was ninety years old and nine, the LORD appeared to Abram, and said unto him, I am the Almighty God; walk before me, and be thou perfect.

GENESIS 17:1 (KJV)

Thou shalt be perfect with the LORD thy God.

DEUTERONOMY 18:13 (KJV)

As for God, His way is perfect; The word of the LORD is proven; He is a shield to all who trust in Him. For who is God, except the LORD? And who is a rock, except our God? God is my strength and power, And He makes my way perfect.

2 SAMUEL 22:31–33 (NKJV)

Therefore you shall be perfect, just as your Father in heaven is perfect.

MATTHEW 5:48 (NKJV)

Him we preach, warning every man and teaching every man in all wisdom, that we may present every man perfect in Christ Jesus.

COLOSSIANS 1:28 (NKJV)

And He Himself gave some to be apostles, some prophets, some evangelists, and some pastors and teachers, for the equipping of the saints for the work of ministry, for the edifying of the body of Christ, till we all come to the unity of the faith and of the knowledge of the Son of God, to a perfect man, to the measure of the stature of the fullness of Christ;

EPHESIANS 4:11–13 (NKJV)

Therefore, having these promises, beloved, let us cleanse ourselves from all filthiness of the flesh and spirit, perfecting holiness in the fear of God.

2 CORINTHIANS 7:1 (NKJV)

> For we are glad, when we are weak, and ye are strong: and this also we wish, even your perfection. Therefore I write these things being absent, lest being present I should use sharpness, according to the power which the Lord hath given me to edification, and not to destruction. Finally, brethren, farewell. Be perfect, be of good comfort, be of one mind, live in peace; and the God of love and peace shall be with you.
>
> 2 Corinthians 13:9–11 (KJV)

> But let patience have its perfect work, that you may be perfect and complete, lacking nothing.
>
> James 1:4 (NKJV)

From Genesis to Revelation, God's desire and command for mankind is to be perfect. Well, just how "perfect" are we expected to be? Just as perfect as our "Father in heaven is perfect" and just as perfect as "the measure of the stature of the fullness of Christ."

If you are thinking, "Wow! You've got to be kidding!" or "No way!" then you are where I was when I first read Jesus's commandment. I thought, "There must be some way around the plain text meaning." Perhaps the Greek word translated as *perfect* in each of the New Testament passages has an alternative in its range of meaning, which would be a little less challenging. Well, as it turns out, the Greek word *teleios*, "τέλειος does have an alternate meaning of "complete."[1] Unfortunately, being as complete as God the Father is complete does nothing to diminish the command. In the end, I realized that my heart was wrong in trying to "get out of" the plain text meaning. I discovered that the appropriate response was to find out why God felt he had given man a legitimate and attainable command and just what constituted this "perfection" that God was expecting of his followers.

I began by asking what constituted *perfection* in God's lexicon. God is both the definer and the definition of *perfection*. He has given us his standards of perfection in the Scriptures. He has defined what is just, righteous, gracious, loving, truthful, faithful, and godly. He has outlined what is right and wrong in interpersonal and international relations. He has described and exemplified true religion and condemned all false religions and religious practices. He has defined himself as the truth (John 14:6) and the embodiment of perfection, and he has denounced all counterclaims as deceptions and lies (Isaiah 42:5–8, 43:9–13). Note what Jesus says about this issue: "The disciple is not above his master: but every one that is perfect shall be as his master" (Luke 6:40, KJV). The bottom line is this: Jesus *is* God's definition of perfection. We are to be just like Jesus in our attitude and our works. Just as Paul explains in Ephesians 4:13 above, this is the goal of every individual in the Church: pastor, elder, and laymen alike. Further, it is the responsibility of every apostle, prophet, evangelist, pastor, and teacher in the church to proclaim this standard and work for it until all become the very likeness of Jesus Christ.

Now before you shrug this off as the musings of some idealistic missionary who has totally lost control of reality, let me see if I can lay out the sequence of events and purposes which, from God's point of view, makes his commandment imperative, attainable, and logical. Remember, at the beginning I said that we would look at God's perspective on this issue. In order to understand his point of view, we had to look at his purposes in Jesus Christ, the Holy Spirit, and man. When we see what he has done to enable man to live the type of life that he commands, then it becomes easier to accept his standard and decide whether we are willing to pursue it so that his kingdom might come on earth as it is in heaven, as we frequently pray. If we refuse God's plan, then we will move inexorably toward global destruction as described in Revelation. The church will sink further into the likeness of the Laodicean church, ready to be vomited out of God's mouth (Revelation 3:14–19).

But, like Paul, I'm persuaded of better things from those of us who love Jesus (Hebrews 6:9–12). Let us therefore move on to perfection (Hebrew 6:1–2) and look at how God removed all but one of the obstacles to this goal and personally empowered believers to live in joyful and loving harmony with all mankind. A synoptic summary of these actions follows:

## God's Plan Revisited

We have come a long way to get to this point. We have looked at God's purposes for sending his Son Jesus the Christ, his purposes for sending the Holy Spirit, and his purposes for his greatest earthly creation, man. We have reviewed scriptures from Genesis to Revelation that unlock several keys to understanding God's plans, commands, and character. We have done all this, as I mentioned at the very beginning, to come to an understanding of God's perspicacious provisions for man's perfection. We have done all this so that we might understand from God's perspective why he feels that his command for man to be perfect is both legitimate and attainable by every person on earth who will understand and accept his conditions. As man's creator, there is nothing that he does not understand about man's capabilities, problems, or limitations. He completely understands the spiritual world and the war for the hearts and minds of every man, woman, and child on earth. He has sent himself in the Persons of his Son and his Holy Spirit to empower mankind both to understand the battle and to overcome all obstacles to holiness, righteousness, and justice now. The following is a table summarizing what God has done to enable this victorious living in Christ:

| Man's problem | God's solution | Scripture reference |
|---|---|---|
| 1. Unbelief | • Creation itself,<br>• Jesus: truth, author, and finisher of our faith<br>• Holy Spirit: teacher of truth, revealer of Christ<br>• Signs and wonders | • Romans 1:18–20<br>• John 14:6; Hebrew 12:2<br>• John 14:16–17, 26; 15:26; 16:13–14<br>• Mark 16:19–20; Acts |
| 2. Sin<br>• Separation from God<br>• Broken communication<br>• Death, lake of fire<br>• Law of sin | • Define sin<br>• Redeem and reconcile man<br>• Listen to and answer prayers<br>• Abolish death, inaugurate eternal life with him<br>• Law of the Spirit, God's seed in man | • 1 John 3:4; Galatians 5:19–21; 1 John 5:17<br>• Titus 2:11–14; 2 Corinthians 5:18–21<br>• John 15:7, 14:12–14<br>• 2 Timothy 1:10; John 3:16; 1 John 5:11–12<br>• Romans 8:2–4; 1 John 3:9 |
| 3. Ignorance (n.b. Hosea 4:6)<br>• Of the law<br>• Of God's wisdom<br>• Of the truth | • Torah/Pentateuch, Jesus<br>• The wisdom scriptures, Jesus<br>• The Bible, Jesus, Holy Spirit | • Genesis–Deuteronomy; Matthew 5–7 (n.b. 5:17); 2 Corinthians 3:4–9 (n.b. verse 6)<br>• Job–Ecclesiastes (n.b. Proverbs 8); 1 Corinthians 1:30<br>• 2 Timothy 3:16–17; John 14:6,16–17; 2 John 1–2 |

| Man's problem | God's solution | Scripture reference |
|---|---|---|
| • Of God's character | • Psalms, prophets, gospels, Jesus | • Psalms; Isaiah–Malachi; Matthew–John (n.b. 14:7–11; 10:30); Revelation |
| • Of God's dealings with man | • Historical books of the Bible | • Genesis–Ester; Matthew–Acts; etc. |
| • Of God's prophecies | • Prophetic books of the Bible | • Isaiah–Malachi; Matthew–John; Revelation; etc. |
| • Of God's Son, Jesus | • The gospels, theophanies | • Matthew–John; Acts– Revelation; multiple OT visits; |
| • Of God's Holy Spirit | • The new covenant and the New Testament | • Jeremiah 31:31–34 (Hebrews 8–10); Ezekiel 36:26–27; and the NT, esp. Acts 1–2, John 14–16, 1 Corinthians 12–14, Galatians 5, 2 Timothy 3:16, 2 Peter 1:20–21 |
| 4. Satan/demons | • Destroy the works of Satan | • 1 John 3:8; Hebrew 2:14–15 |
| | • Cast out demons | • Luke 9:1; John 14:12; Mark 16:17–18 |
| | • The truth: bring to light all lies and deceptions. | • John 14:6; Mark 4:22; John 8:12; Matthew 5:14–16; 2 Timothy 3:16–17 |
| | • Set the captives free | • John 8:31–36; Isaiah 53:4–12 |
| | • Immunity from satanic attack through sinlessness | • 1 John 5:18 |

| Man's problem | God's solution | Scripture reference |
|---|---|---|
| 5. Death | • The resurrection of Christ<br>• Rebirth in Christ<br>• Translation | • 1 Corinthians 15:3–22, 51–57; 1 John 5:11–12<br>• Galatians 2:20; 2 Corinthians 5:17<br>• Colossians 1:13; Ephesians 2:4–7 |
| 6. Temptation | • Restrict temptation to manageable limits | • 1 Corinthians 10:13; 2 Peter 2:9 |
| 7. Rebellion/ disobedience | • The Holy Spirit<br>• Discipline<br>• Destruction, removal<br>• Reward righteousness | • Ezekiel 36:27<br>• Hebrew 12:3–29<br>• Josh 7:11–26; Ezekiel 18:20–32; Acts 5:1–11<br>• Josh 1:8; Deuteronomy 28:1–14, 8:18–20; Psalm 37:25 |
| 8. Poverty | • Understand contentment and true prosperity/riches | • 1 Timothy 6:6–19; Proverbs 22:1–4; Proverbs 4:5–9 |
| 9. Sickness (all types) | • Reward perfection with health and wholeness<br>• Answer the prayers of the righteous with healing<br>• Give the spiritual gifts of healing and miracles | • Deuteronomy 7:12–15<br>• James 5:14–15; John 14:12–14<br>• 1 Corinthians 12:9–10; Mark 16:20 |
| 10. Guilt | • Forgiveness, redemption, reconciliation, rebirth, the blood | • Hebrews 9:8–15, 22; 2 Corinthians 5:17–21 |

| Man's problem | God's solution | Scripture reference |
|---|---|---|
| | of Jesus, the Holy Spirit | |
| 11. Confusion | • The Truth: Jesus Christ, the Holy Spirit | • John 14:6, 16–17, 26; 1 John 2:26–27; 1 Corinthians 14:26–33 |
| 12. Corrupt government/injustice | • Jesus, the King of kings and Lord of lords<br>• The spirit of his righteous laws, which define justice<br>• Vengeance is mine says the Lord, I will repay<br>• The great commandments | • 1 Timothy 6:13–16<br>• 2 Corinthians 3:6<br>• Romans 12:17–21, esp. 19<br>• Matthew 22:36–40 |
| 13. Pride | • Promotion is from the Lord<br>• Humility | • Psalm 75:6–7; Romans 13:1–7<br>• Matthew 20:25–28; 2 Chronicles 7:14 |
| 14. Power/authority/glory | • Retain it for himself | • Isaiah 42:8, 48:11; Matthew 28:18 |
| 15. Impossibilities<br>• Overcome addictions: drugs, sex, food, money, power, recognition, lying, bad language | • Nothing is impossible for God or Christians<br>• Set the captives free | • Luke 1:37; Mark 9:23; Matthew 17:19–20<br>• Isaiah 61:1–3; 2 Corinthians 5:17; John 8:32–36; Isaiah 53:4–6 |

| Man's problem | God's solution | Scripture reference |
|---|---|---|
| • Righteousness/ holiness/ redemption/ sanctification | • Put the Spirit of Christ in all believers | • Romans 8:9–11; Philippians 1:19–21; 1 Corinthians 1:30; Colossians 1:26–29 |
| • Change bad attitudes | • The mind of Christ | • 1 Corinthians 2:16; Colossians 1:26–29 |
| • Love our enemies/ bless those who curse us/do good to those who hate us/pray for those who despitefully use us and persecute us | • The mind of Christ | • 1 Corinthians 2:16; Colossians 1:26–29 |
| • Salvation from Satan, sin, and death | • Jesus Christ | • Luke 1:69–71; 1 John 3:8–9; 2 Timothy 1:10 |
| • Be released from bondages: spiritual (curses, witchcraft, idolatry, cults, cultic practices, ungodly cultural traditions), physical, and emotional | • Set the captives free | • Isaiah 61:1–3; 2 Corinthians 5:17; John 8:32–36; Isaiah 53:4–6 |
| • Death to self | • Enable man to understand the need and empower him to do the deed | • 1 Corinthians 2:16; Proverbs 9:10; Psalm 119:144; Romans 6:6–7; Colossians 3:1–14; Ephesians 4:20–32; Galatians 2:20; Mark 8:35; Philippians 2:12–13 |

Two things are important to note at this point. First, I know that many of you already love the Lord and have walked with him many years yourselves. You may have other verses that are your favorites, which give additional nuances of understanding and hues of meaning in each of the areas referenced above. The table serves as a foundation for the forthcoming conclusions, not as an exhaustive treatise of the subject. The ones I have chosen are simply some that have enlightened me and given me joy and understanding in each of the areas discussed.

Second, it is hard to plumb the depths of God's knowledge, wisdom, and judgment. It's like taking your bass fishing depth-finder to the Philippine Trench. I am well aware of the following passages:

> Let the wicked forsake his way, And the unrighteous man his thoughts; Let him return to the LORD, And He will have mercy on him; And to our God, For He will abundantly pardon. "For My thoughts are not your thoughts, Nor are your ways My ways," says the LORD. "For as the heavens are higher than the earth, So are My ways higher than your ways, And My thoughts than your thoughts. For as the rain comes down, and the snow from heaven, And do not return there, But water the earth, And make it bring forth and bud, That it may give seed to the sower And bread to the eater, So shall My word be that goes forth from My mouth; It shall not return to Me void, But it shall accomplish what I please, And it shall prosper in the thing for which I sent it."
>
> Isaiah 55:7–11 (NKJV)

> Oh, the depth of the riches both of the wisdom and knowledge of God! How unsearchable are His judgments and His ways past finding out! For who has known the mind of the LORD? Or who has become His counselor? Or who has first given to Him And it shall be repaid to him? For of Him and through Him and to Him are all things, to whom be glory forever. Amen.
>
> Romans 11:33–36 (NKJV)

I mention these passages by way of humility and to note that the perfection that God expects of mankind is not perfection of knowledge, wisdom, or understanding. When Paul says that we have the mind of Christ, he is not meaning to imply that we have the entire wisdom and knowledge base of God. We do not and cannot. We do not perfectly understand cell physiology, genetics, biochemistry, physics, atomic structure, meteorology, climatology, astronomy, psychology, economics, and a whole host of other disciplines. But this is not the point. The perfection that God is requiring of man is perfection of attitude and behavior toward him and his creation, especially mankind. Specifically, he defines *perfection* as having the attitudes and behavior of Jesus Christ in his capacity as a man. He wants us to willingly and joyfully emulate Christ's righteousness and holiness. After all, it is Christ who works in us both to will and to do of his good pleasure! (Philippians 2:13)

If you will study and meditate on each of the scriptures referenced in the table above, I believe you'll come to an understanding of God's point of view with regard to his command that we be perfect. He is not asking us to do something that is impossible or that would frustrate us to death. All that he has required from us he has empowered us to accomplish or exemplify through his Son Jesus Christ and the gift of his Holy Spirit.

Furthermore, he's not giving us an arbitrary command. He clearly understands that if man is left to the impulses of his sinful nature, he will seek power to dominate and oppress others for his own selfish purposes. History is replete with records of man's inhumanity to man and his capacity to do evil. God understands both the source and the power of this evil. He stepped into history precisely for the purpose of revealing these things and of saving man from them. That is why Jesus is called the Light of the World and our Savior. No darkness can hide from the Light, and no evil can overcome the good.

So you historians ponder this: I know of no government that has ever been able to provide its people sustained peace, harmony, and prosperity in the absence of absolutely righteous leaders. Consider them all: monarchies, dictatorships, republics, democracies, socialist states, communist states, oligarchies, etc. Consider the different philosophers: Socrates, Plato, Tao, Confucius, Kant, Marx, Sartre, de Tocqueville, Nietzsche, Kierkegaard, Mills, etc. Which has been able to define the perfect way to righteousness and holiness and to empower his followers to be righteous and holy in order to benefit all of society? Without the God of the Bible, no system of governance has worked. It cannot. Why? Because none of these others has dealt with man's sinful nature. None disembowels his innate wickedness and selfishness. None neutralizes man's desperately wicked heart. Consequently no laws, no matter how righteous or well enforced, can make men be good. No religion, no matter how righteous its laws or disciplined its followers, has the power to overcome man's sinful nature. That is why Judaism, without Jesus or the Holy Spirit, failed to change the hearts of the Hebrews. That is why the Jews failed to bring righteousness and holiness into this world, although God himself had given them righteous laws and had been their protector and guide. Without squarely addressing the problem of his fallen nature, man will use cunning and deceit to look for loopholes in laws and to manipulate rules and ordinances for his own selfish purposes. Hence, graft and corruption of all kinds proliferate in governments and civil institutions, fomenting lawlessness, cheating, and oppression.

The problem, beloved, is our heart and our mind, our attitude and our will. The new covenant changed both. God gave us a new heart, and he wrote his laws on our heart and our mind. Then he put his Holy Spirit within us, and he caused us to walk in his statutes and to keep his commandments. We no longer *have to* keep his laws: we *want to* keep them. We don't *try* to do what is right and good: we are *empowered* to do what is right and good. This transaction represents a complete paradigm shift, a complete change of worldview. It's what Jesus called being born again: old things have passed away, behold, all things have become new. Our old, sinful nature has been crucified, and our new life in Christ has begun. What made perfection impossible in the past, God has made possible in the present.

This total change of mind and heart and concomitant empowerment to live righteously are God's solutions to the world's problems of sin, hatred, strife, envy, immorality, murder, war, unforgiveness, Satan and his minions, etc. There's only one thing that is holding those who call themselves Christians back from realizing the power of this conversion and the resultant positive impact that it could have on the church, the family, the workplace, the government, and the world. What is that one thing? Death to self.

God does not force anyone to be a Christian or behave like one. He will not kill our old, sinful nature. The Bible says that that is our decision and our responsibility (e.g., Mark 8:34–35; Luke 11:13; Ephesians 4:22–24; Colossians 3:2–14; etc.). God has empowered every Christian to be perfect and to have a tremendous impact for good in society. Salvation and rebirth are God's free gift of grace to all who will receive it. Most who call themselves Christians already know this and have invited Christ into their life to be their Lord and Savior. What most do not know is that they must finish the transaction by willingly crucifying their sinful nature, putting off the old man. If they don't, they will have an internal power struggle ala Romans 6–7 over who is the real Lord of their life: Jesus, the old man (self), or some deception or idol.

## The Signs of Perfection

At this point some of you may be asking yourselves, "What are the pragmatic evidences of a perfected Christian life today? What does a perfect Christian look like?" The answer is profoundly simple: Jesus Christ. Consider what the scriptures have to say about these questions:

> Now by this we know that we know Him, if we keep His commandments. He who says, "I know Him," and does not keep His commandments, is a liar, and the truth is not in him. But whoever keeps His word, truly the love of God is perfected in him. By this we know that we are in Him. He who says he abides in Him ought himself also to walk just as He walked.
>
> 1 John 2:3–6 (NKJV)

> Beware of false prophets, who come to you in sheep's clothing, but inwardly they are ravenous wolves. You will know them by their fruits. Do men gather grapes from thorn bushes or figs from thistles? Even so, every good tree bears good fruit, but a bad tree bears bad fruit. A good tree cannot bear bad fruit, nor can a bad tree bear good fruit. Every tree that does not bear good fruit is cut down and thrown into the fire. Therefore by their fruits you will know them.
>
> Matthew 7:15–20 (NKJV)

> A disciple is not above his teacher, nor a servant above his master. It is enough for a disciple that he be like his teacher, and a servant like his master.
>
> Matthew 10:24–25 (NKJV)

From the above, it is clear that the first sign of perfection in a Christian is that he walks just as Christ walked, that he is like his teacher, and that he bears good fruit. It does not mean that he is a Jesus clone. No one has been given all of the spiritual gifts Christ was given as the only begotten Son of God. It simply means that he exhibits the same character and attitudes as his Teacher and that the works of his life manifest righteousness and holiness in the utilization of the spiritual gift or gifts that he has been given by God. It means that he is a new creation in Christ Jesus, that he is Spirit-baptized and Spirit-filled, that he is a new covenant member of the body of Christ (the church), that his old, sinful nature has been crucified with Christ, and that he's been translated into the kingdom of God. It means that he has been saved, redeemed, reconciled, raised, and adopted by God; that all the promises of God are his; that he is a mighty, victorious warrior for his Lord; and that Christ always causes him to triumph. That's just to recount the basics. If these things don't bring joy to your heart and a rejoicing to your spirit, it is simply because you have not researched the Scriptures and allowed the blessings of these truths to gladden your spirit.

## Walk as He Walked

So walking as he walked is the first evidence of a perfected life in Christ. And like a perfectly cut diamond, this "walking" has many facets and a kaleidoscope of colors. So before leaving this topic, I would like to share a few more scriptures that deal with the issue of "walking." Please consider the following:

> But the fruit of the Spirit is love, joy, peace, longsuffering, kindness, goodness, faithfulness, gentleness, self-control. Against such there is no law. And those who are Christ's have crucified the flesh with its passions and desires. If we live in the Spirit, let us also walk in the Spirit. Let us not become conceited, provoking one another, envying one another.
>
> GALATIANS 5:22–25 (NKJV)

> Therefore we were buried with Him through baptism into death, that just as Christ was raised from the dead by the glory of the Father, even so we also should walk in newness of life.
>
> ROMANS 6:4 (NKJV)

> There is therefore now no condemnation to those who are in Christ Jesus, who do not walk according to the flesh, but according to the Spirit. For the law of the Spirit of life in Christ Jesus has made me free from the law of sin and death. For what the law could not do in that it was weak through the flesh, God did by sending His own Son in the

likeness of sinful flesh, on account of sin: He condemned sin in the flesh, that the righteous requirement of the law might be fulfilled in us who do not walk according to the flesh but according to the Spirit.

ROMANS 8:1–4 (NKJV)

Let us walk properly, as in the day, not in revelry and drunkenness, not in lewdness and lust, not in strife and envy.

ROMANS 13:13 (NKJV)

But as God has distributed to each one, as the Lord has called each one, so let him walk. And so I ordain in all the churches.

1 CORINTHIANS 7:17 (NKJV)

I say then: Walk in the Spirit, and you shall not fulfill the lust of the flesh.

GALATIANS 5:16 (NKJV)

For we are His workmanship, created in Christ Jesus for good works, which God prepared beforehand that we should walk in them.

EPHESIANS 2:10 (NKJV)

This I say, therefore, and testify in the Lord, that you should no longer walk as the rest of the Gentiles walk, in the futility of their mind, having their understanding darkened, being alienated from the life of God, because of the ignorance that is in them, because of the blindness of their heart; who, being past feeling, have given themselves over to lewdness, to work all uncleanness with greediness.

EPHESIANS 4:17–19 (NKJV)

And walk in love, as Christ also has loved us and given Himself for us, an offering and a sacrifice to God for a sweet-smelling aroma.

EPHESIANS 5:2 (NKJV)

For you were once darkness, but now you are light in the Lord. Walk as children of light.

Ephesians 5:8 (NKJV)

As you have therefore received Christ Jesus the Lord, so walk in Him.

Colossians 2:6 (NKJV)

Walk in wisdom toward those who are outside, redeeming the time.

Colossians 4:5 (NKJV)

If we say that we have fellowship with Him, and walk in darkness, we lie and do not practice the truth. But if we walk in the light as He is in the light, we have fellowship with one another, and the blood of Jesus Christ His Son cleanses us from all sin.

1 John 1:6–7 (NKJV)

This is love, that we walk according to His commandments. This is the commandment, that as you have heard from the beginning, you should walk in it.

2 John 1:6 (NKJV)

For I rejoiced greatly when brethren came and testified of the truth that is in you, just as you walk in the truth. I have no greater joy than to hear that my children walk in truth.

3 John 3–4 (NKJV)

Who is wise? Let him understand these things. Who is prudent? Let him know them. For the ways of the LORD are right; The righteous walk in them, But transgressors stumble in them.

Hosea 14:9 (NKJV)

I will put My Spirit within you and cause you to walk in My statutes, and you will keep My judgments and do them.

Ezekiel 36:27 (NKJV)

> Blessed is the man who walks not in the counsel of the ungodly, Nor stands in the path of sinners, Nor sits in the seat of the scornful; But his delight is in the law of the LORD, And in His law he meditates day and night. He shall be like a tree Planted by the rivers of water, That brings forth its fruit in its season, Whose leaf also shall not wither; And whatever he does shall prosper. The ungodly are not so, But are like the chaff which the wind drives away.
>
> Psalm 1:1–4 (NKJV)

Wow! The above may seem like a lot of verses, but the truth is that this is only a sampling of the many verses in Scripture that ask Christians to walk in ways pleasing to God. Our words and actions are to reflect the attributes of our Lord and bring honor and glory to his name. Our studies, our athletic behavior, our business dealings, our family relationships, our judgments, our governments, our integrity, our industry, and all our interpersonal relationships should reflect the wisdom and righteousness of God.

Some may object that this amounts to works of righteousness, pleading Ephesians 2:8–9. To this I would reply with Ephesians 2:10, the very next verse and the argument of James. Verse 10 states that we are God's workmanship created in Christ to do the *good works* that God has before ordained that we should do. As born-again Christians, God truly does have a plan for our life. Each Christian is valuable and has a purpose. We're not to bury our God-given gifts; we are to use them for his glory and for the benefit of other people (Matthew 25:14–30, esp. 25).

Further, this is not just a salvation issue, but it is also a proof issue. James challenges his readers with this text: "Show me your faith without your works, and I will show you my faith by my works. But do you want to know, O foolish man, that faith without works is dead?" (James 2:18, 20, NKJV).

Even Paul admonished:

> Therefore, my beloved, as you have always obeyed, not only in my presence, but now much more in my absence, work out your own salvation with fear and trembling. For it is God Who works in you both to will and to do of His good pleasure. Do all things without murmurings and disputings, that you may be blameless and harmless, children of God, without rebuke, in the midst of a crooked and perverse nation, among whom you shine as lights in the world.
>
> PHILIPPIANS 2:12–15 (NKJV)

Clearly, we are to work out what God has worked in. We are to be and to do what God has empowered us to be and do through his Son and Holy Spirit.

Finally, contrary to much of today's candy-coated theology, works *are* part of the salvation equation. Consider the following words of our Lord Jesus:

> Not everyone who says to Me, "Lord, Lord," shall enter the kingdom of heaven, *but he who does the will of My Father in heaven.* Many will say to Me in that day, "Lord, Lord, have we not prophesied in Your name, cast out demons in Your name, and done many wonders in Your name?" And then I will declare to them, "I never knew you; depart from Me, you who practice lawlessness!"
>
> MATTHEW 7:21–23 (NKJV, ITALICS MINE)

> For I say to you, that unless your righteousness exceeds the righteousness of the scribes and Pharisees, you will by no means enter the kingdom of heaven. [cf. Philippians 3:4–9; 1 Corinthians 4:1–5]
>
> MATTHEW 5:20 (NKJV)

Review Revelation 2 and 3 and note how Jesus judges the seven churches. To each one he says, "I know your works…" and "to him who overcomes …." He judges their works first and then rewards only those who overcome their sinful issues. Remember as you carefully review each case that Jesus is addressing church members and ponder the things that he judges in each one. (n.b. 3:1–5, 14–19)

> And He said to me, "It is done! I am the Alpha and the Omega, the Beginning and the End. I will give of the fountain of the water of life freely to him who thirsts. He who overcomes shall inherit all things, and I will be his God and he shall be My son. But the cowardly, unbelieving, abominable, murderers, sexually immoral, sorcerers, idolaters, and all liars shall have their part in the lake which burns with fire and brimstone, which is the second death."
>
> Revelation 21:6–8 (NKJV)

To these verses, John and Peter, by the Holy Spirit, add the following:

> And I saw the dead, small and great, standing before God, and books were opened. And another book was opened, which is the Book of Life. And the dead were judged according to their works, by the things which were written in the books. The sea gave up the dead who were in it, and Death and Hades delivered up the dead who were in them. And they were judged, each one according to his works. Then Death and Hades were cast into the lake of fire. This is the second death. And anyone not found written in the Book of Life was cast into the lake of fire.
>
> Revelation 20:12–15 (NKJV)

> And if you call on the Father, who without partiality judges according to each one's work, conduct yourselves throughout the time of your stay here in fear.
>
> 1 Peter 1:17 (NKJV)

This last verse is most assuredly addressed to believers, and it highlights both the principle of works and the fear of the Lord for believers. Christians are to walk their talk. Failure of Christians to do so has caused many to stumble.

Let me give you a personal glimpse of the problem with sin permeating a national church. Consider the compromised testimony of the Philippines. Jackie and I were missionaries there for thirteen years, and God placed a genuine love of the people in our hearts. At first, we wondered to ourselves why God would want to send us as missionaries to the only Christian nation in Asia. It was only after we arrived that we discovered that the Philippines was also the secondmost corrupt nation in Asia! Wow! How do you think God feels about that? How much positive influence do you think the Philippines has spiritually in Asia with that kind of reputation? When adultery, fornication, lying, stealing, murder, bribery, alcoholism, marital dysfunction, idolatry, cults, voodoo, and other cultic practices thrive beside and within the church, what kind of a testimony does that give? We rapidly discovered God's purpose for our being there.

The sad truth, however, is that we don't need to look at Asia or the Philippines to find the same kinds of problems. When our nation produces and exports movies and television programs with cursing, adultery, fornication, homosexuality, abortion, pornography, violence, and satanic content, what is our testimony to the world? What kind of respect do we expect to receive from developing countries when our entertainment is pure trash, our economic house is in disarray, immorality abounds, our leaders hold truth in subordination to political correctness and expedience, our business leaders are covetous and often oppressors, and our church leaders are more interested in prosperity and getting people "saved" than they are in holiness and righteousness?

Works do matter! How we live and what we say does matter! Beloved, God is counting on us. He has invested his Son and his Holy Spirit in a world that he has created and he loves. He has not created it to be a hellhole of misery and tears. He has created it to be a beautiful place of love, respect, righteousness, holiness, and truth. And he has sent his Son and Holy Spirit to enable mankind to come back to that vision and to live it. He has come to earth; has taught us the truth; has established his kingdom and righteousness; has washed away our sins in the blood of his Son Jesus; has reconciled us to himself as a loving Father to a wayward child; has adopted us as his own children; has given us a new heart, a new mind, and a new Spirit; has defeated Satan, sin, and death; and has empowered us to do the same in our lives. Concomitantly, he has filled us with this Holy Spirit so that we may be set free from all addictions and deceptions through knowing the truth and walking in the truth. Further, his Holy Spirit has empowered Christians with fruits and gifts to walk as he walked. The church, as the body of Christ, was to collectively represent and provide to the world the fullness of the love and giftings of Jesus Christ. This was and is God's perfect plan for redeeming and empowering man to be the righteous overseer of the world that he originally created him, in his image, to be.

So let's be honest and fair: just what more does man expect God to do? He has done everything to enable him to be reconciled to himself and to function lovingly and righteously on earth. The only thing he has not done is forced man to be good. He has not made us robots. He has not been a dictatorial tyrant. Perfect love does not behave in that way.

And anyway, the first and great commandment rings a little hollow if there are no options for man. God's command that we love him with all of our heart and soul and mind and strength would seem a bit gratuitous if we had no options. Love must be earned, not forced. Through creation, his word, his actions through history, his Son's sacrifice, his Holy Spirit, and his benevolent promises, he has demonstrated his love for us and has more than earned our genuine gratitude and our unfeigned love (John 3:16; Romans 5:8). Truly, we do love him because he first loved us (1 John 4:19).

## Love as He Loved

All this brings us to the most important attribute of genuine Christians: agape love. Love is the sine qua non of Christianity. Paul, by the Spirit, wrote the following: "But above all these things put on love, which is the bond of perfection" (Colossians 3:14, NKJV). The statement is all the more powerful considering the fact that he has just said, "You have put off the old man with his deeds, and have put on the new man." He is asserting here that putting on love is even more important than putting off our old, sinful behavior and putting on righteous behavior. Why? Because love gets at the heart of our motivation for being righteous. It is not enough to be blameless in our actions: God wants us also to be faultless in our motives.

Before moving on, however, we must deal with the semantic issues of *love. Love* is a very slippery word in English. We can say that we "love" to walk, to read, to sing, etc. Here, the word *love* can be translated as "like a lot" or "like most of all." We can also say that "they are making love" when we mean that they are engaging in sexual intercourse. Or we can say, "I love my mom and dad, sister, friend, etc.," when we are expressing familial or brotherly affection. These are all valid uses of the word *love*, but none captures the distinctive character of the Greek word *agape* (ἀγάπη) or its verbal form, *agapao*, which are translated "love" or "to love" in most modern English translations. Unlike contemporary English, the biblical Greek language has distinctive words that convey the different nuances of love mentioned above. The radical difference in *agape* is that it is an others-centered love. Each of the other forms of love is typically a self-centered expression of affection. As mentioned earlier, that is why many feel that the King James rendering of agape as "charity" more closely defines the appropriate Greek nuance than the conventional *love*. Paul gives the best biblical description of this love in the following:

> Love suffers long and is kind; love does not envy; love does not parade itself, is not puffed up; does not behave rudely, does not seek its own, is not provoked, thinks no evil; does not rejoice in iniquity, but rejoices in the truth; bears all things, believes all things, hopes all things, endures all things. Love never fails. But whether there are prophecies, they will fail; whether there are tongues, they will cease; whether there is knowledge, it will vanish away.
>
> 1 CORINTHIANS 13:4–8 (NKJV)

Linguistics aside, the important thing to remember is that in each of the following passages and verses, the word that is used for *love* in the Greek is *agape* or *agapao*, and each refers to others-centered, godly love. Truly, this agape love is the central issue of Christianity. Let me show you why.

## Knowing God Depends on Love

> Beloved, let us love one another, for love is of God; and everyone who loves is born of God and knows God. He who does not love does not know God, for God is love.
>
> 1 JOHN 4:7–8 (NKJV)

Notice first that *agape* love is "of God," literally "out of the God." It is not a natural love of man; it is a supernatural love given to all who are born of him and know him. Anyone who does not have this others-centered love does not know God, because his very nature is love.

## Love Is the Action Required in Both Great Commandments

> Jesus said to him, "You shall love the LORD your God with all your heart, with all your soul, and with all your mind. This is the first and great commandment. And the second is like it: 'You shall love your neighbor as yourself.' On these two commandments hang all the Law and the Prophets."
>
> MATTHEW 22:37–40 (NKJV)

Jesus is saying here that almost the entire Old Testament can be summarized by two commandments: love God completely and love your neighbor as yourself. In both of these commandments, the action required is agape love, and it is only through this lens of love that these commands and the actions of God in the Bible can be understood and interpreted. If we keep these commandments from the heart, then justice, righteousness, peace, and prosperity will follow.

## Love Is the Action Required in Jesus's New Commandment

> A new commandment I give to you, that you love one another; as I have loved you, that you also love one another. By this all will know that you are My disciples, if you have love for one another.
>
> JOHN 13:34–35 (NKJV)

> If someone says, "I love God," and hates his brother, he is a liar; for he who does not love his brother whom he has seen, how can he love God whom he has not seen? And this commandment we have from Him: that he who loves God must love his brother also.
>
> 1 JOHN 4:20–21 (NKJV)

The distinctive feature of the disciple of Jesus Christ is that he exhibits a selfless love for his fellow Christians, a love of the same nature and kind as Jesus exhibited to each of his disciples. This love involved teaching, training, encouraging, correcting, listening, healing, forgiving, empowering, sympathizing, empathizing, being patient, being self-controlled, and going the extra mile in several other spiritual areas. In the end, it meant giving his life for them. And "greater love has no man than this: that he lay down his life for his friends" (John 15:13, KJV). This type of love does not come naturally to man. It is a supernatural empowerment of the nature of God, which he commands each of his followers to exercise. It is the first fruit of the Holy Spirit who indwells every born-again believer who asks for him (Luke 11:13; Galatians 5:22).

## Love Is the Motivation and Empowerment to Keep God's Commandments

> Whoever believes that Jesus is the Christ is born of God, and everyone who loves Him who begot also loves him who is begotten of Him. By this we know that we love the children of God, when we love God and keep His commandments. For this is the love of God, that we keep His commandments. And His commandments are not burdensome. For whatever is born of God overcomes the world. And this is the victory that has overcome the world—our faith.
>
> 1 JOHN 5:1–4 (NKJV)

> If you love Me, keep My commandments.
>
> JOHN 14:15 (NKJV)

> He who has My commandments and keeps them, it is he who loves Me. And he who loves Me will be loved by My Father, and I will love him and manifest Myself to him.
>
> JOHN 14:21 (NKJV)

> He who says, "I know Him," and does not keep His commandments, is a liar, and the truth is not in him. But whoever keeps His word, truly the love of God is perfected in him. By this we know that we are in Him. He who says he abides in Him ought himself also to walk just as He walked.
>
> 1 JOHN 2:4–6 (NKJV)

From the above it is clear that we cannot say that we're born-again Christians just because we go to church every Sunday, call Jesus "Lord," raise up our hands in praise and worship, kneel humbly in the pew and recite memorized prayers, give of our time and money, sit on a church board, teach at a seminary, or preach in a church. God does not ask us to look like Christians: he asks us to be like his Son, Jesus Christ, and to demonstrate that love by wholeheartedly submitting to his will as expressed in his commandments, his imperative statements, and his word delivered to his personally chosen and called apostles and prophets. Born-again Christians will not balk at this, resent it, rebel against it, ignore it, or try to rationalize it. They will simply and humbly submit and obey because they know the character of God and trust the wisdom and love that he has not only for them but for others as well. They realize that God is wiser than they are and that he knows best about how people can relate righteously, justly, and peaceably with one another. Further, they know that the manifestation of an agape love in an individual demonstrates that God's love is perfected in him or her.

The following commandments, which are difficult or impossible for the natural man, can only be understood and heartily obeyed through the indwelling agape love and wisdom of God.

> But I say to you, love your enemies, bless those who curse you, do good to those who hate you, and pray for those who spitefully use you and persecute you.
>
> MATTHEW 5:44 (NKJV)

> Repay no one evil for evil. Have regard for good things in the sight of all men. If it is possible, as much as depends on you, live peaceably with all men. Beloved, do not avenge yourselves, but rather give place to wrath; for it is written, "Vengeance is Mine, I will repay," says the Lord. Therefore "If your enemy is hungry, feed him; If he is thirsty, give him a drink; For in so doing you will heap coals of fire on his head." Do not be overcome by evil, but overcome evil with good.
>
> ROMANS 12:17–21 (NKJV)

Wives, submit to your own husbands, as to the Lord. For the husband is head of the wife, as also Christ is head of the church; and He is the Savior of the body. Therefore, just as the church is subject to Christ, so let the wives be to their own husbands in everything.

Ephesians 5:22–24 (NKJV)

Husbands, love your wives, just as Christ also loved the church and gave Himself for her, that He might sanctify and cleanse her with the washing of water by the word, that He might present her to Himself a glorious church, not having spot or wrinkle or any such thing, but that she should be holy and without blemish. So husbands ought to love their own wives as their own bodies; he who loves his wife loves himself.

Ephesians 5:25–28 (NKJV)

Let your women keep silent in the churches, for they are not permitted to speak; but they are to be submissive, as the law also says. And if they want to learn something, let them ask their own husbands at home; for it is shameful for women to speak in church. Or did the word of God come originally from you? Or was it you only that it reached? If anyone thinks himself to be a prophet or spiritual, let him acknowledge that the things which I write to you are the commandments of the Lord.

1 Corinthians 14:34–37 (NKJV)

Therefore you shall be perfect, just as your Father in heaven is perfect.

Matthew 5:48 (NKJV)

He who says he abides in Him ought himself also to walk just as He walked.

1 John 2:6 (NKJV)

These are just a few of the commandments of God that challenge the credulity of man. To some, they may seem pious but impossible statements. Some are offended or challenged by their hierarchical content or their seeming oversight of "justice." It is precisely at these times when it is necessary to submit to the will of God and trust in his wisdom. It is the time when our agape love for God yields in humility to his expressed will and seeks through the mind of Christ to discern God's reasons for his commands and his plans. Nevertheless, even if our reasoning is unfruitful or our pleas unheard, we will conclude, as Jesus did with drops of blood dripping in the garden of Gethsemane, "Nevertheless, not My will but Thy will be done." God does not always answer the questions why, how fair is that, or isn't there another way? He doesn't have to. Faith, hope, and love answer them. Frequently, history and experience also affirm their wisdom and righteousness.

## Love Is the Motivation of Mercy and Grace

> Hatred stirs up strife, But love covers all sins.
>
> PROVERBS 10:12 (NKJV)

> He who covers a transgression seeks love, But he who repeats a matter separates friends.
>
> PROVERBS 17:9 (NKJV)

> And above all things have fervent love for one another, for love will cover a multitude of sins.
>
> 1 PETER 4:8 (NKJV)

> For God so loved the world that He gave His only begotten Son, that whoever believes in Him should not perish but have everlasting life.
>
> JOHN 3:16 (NKJV)

> Now hope does not disappoint, because the love of God has been poured out in our hearts by the Holy Spirit who was given to us. For when we were still without strength, in due time Christ died for the ungodly. For scarcely for a righteous man will one die; yet perhaps for

> a good man someone would even dare to die. But God demonstrates His own love toward us, in that while we were still sinners, Christ died for us. Much more then, having now been justified by His blood, we shall be saved from wrath through Him. For if when we were enemies we were reconciled to God through the death of His Son, much more, having been reconciled, we shall be saved by His life. And not only that, but we also rejoice in God through our Lord Jesus Christ, through whom we have now received the reconciliation.
>
> ROMANS 5:5–11 (NKJV)

Jesus Christ is the perfect example of how agape love covers all sins. None of us needs to be told that hatred stirs up strife; we've all seen it. The world is full of hatred and strife. What each of us longs to know and to understand is what to do about it. How can we get over bitterness, envy, vengeance, hatred, and war? How can polarized families, tribes, nations, cultures, and philosophies be reconciled? God gives us the answer, and it begins with agape love.

Agape love is what enables man to love his neighbors as himself and to live in unity and harmony with them. It fills him with mercy and grace. It enables him to cover all sins by forgiving from the heart, by canceling all debts, and by leaving all judgment and vengeance, if any, to God. It enables reconciliation of the most intransigent foes. It superimposes God's kingdom culture over every local, tribal, or national culture. This is the work of Jesus Christ and his Holy Spirit in each and every individual who receives him. It is the consummate answer to Jesus's high priestly prayer:

> And for their sakes I sanctify Myself, that they also may be sanctified by the truth. I do not pray for these alone, but also for those who will believe in Me through their word; that they all may be one, as You, Father, are in Me, and I in You; that they also may be one in Us, that the world may believe that You sent Me. And the glory which You gave Me I have given them, that they may be one just as We are one: I in them, and You in Me; that they may be made perfect in one, and that

> the world may know that You have sent Me, and have loved them as You have loved Me.
>
> JOHN 17:19–23 (NKJV)

Truly, no one can be a born-again Christian without agape love. It is not possible in the flesh to forgive rape, murder, the holocaust, ethnic cleansing, political massacres, or other heinous crimes. The old man cries out for vengeance and justice. Even God gets angry with sin. The problem is that anger, punishment, retribution, and *lex talionis* have never solved the problem of man's desperately wicked heart. "Tit for tat" has no end or reconciliation.

Enter God's solution: Jesus Christ and the Holy Spirit. His grace, mercy, and love covered our sins, changed our minds, and reconciled us to himself. Then his abiding presence within empowered us to extend the same agape love to others. Through the mercy and grace extended to us, we now do the same for others, forgiving them and accepting the consequences of that forgiveness. We love others without expecting anything in return. We leave all vengeance and judgment to God. This allows God to do his will by changing our hearts first and by encouraging and empowering us to pray that he will do the same for others as we share the gospel message.

## Love Is the Motivation for Ministry

> So when they had eaten breakfast, Jesus said to Simon Peter, "Simon, son of Jonah, do you love Me more than these?" He said to Him, "Yes, Lord; You know that I love You." He said to him, "Feed My lambs." He said to him again a second time, "Simon, son of Jonah, do you love Me?" He said to Him, "Yes, Lord; You know that I love You." He said to him, "Tend My sheep." He said to him the third time, "Simon, son of Jonah, do you love Me?" Peter was grieved because He said to him the third time, "Do you love Me?" And he said to Him, "Lord, You

> know all things; You know that I love You." Jesus said to him, "Feed My sheep."
>
> JOHN 21:15–17 (NKJV)

Much has been said about the repetition of the questions and the words used in reply, so I will not dwell on these issues here. Suffice it to note that Jesus was not content with a simple "I love you" from Peter. Neither is he content for his servants to make a light response to this penetrating question today.

Two elements of his questioning stand out: (1) do you *agapao* me? and (2) how much do you *agapao* me? Some analysts will point out that Peter never did say that he "*agapao*-ed" Jesus. All three times he responded using the Greek verb *fileo* (φιλέω[2]), meaning brotherly love. Perhaps it's because he had not yet been baptized in the Spirit and honestly felt a deep brotherly affection more than a selfless love for him. Whether or not that's true, the third time Jesus asks the question he uses the same verb Peter did: "Peter, do you even love me as a brother?" Grieved at the repetition and the subtle change of tone he replies, "Lord, you know all things; you know that I love [*fileo*] you."

Before commissioning for ministry, the Lord will always look for the answer to this question, because ministry without genuine love of the Lord is hypocrisy. It is the supernatural love of God that gives the believer the power to overcome trials, persecutions, and temptations, and to persevere with joy and hope in the assigned task.

But the soul-searching question about the quality of our love for Jesus is only the first part of the query. The second part of Jesus' question was equally penetrating: "Peter, do you love me more than these guys?" It was like asking a boot camp trainee if he loved his drill sergeant more than his comrades. Peter had gone through three solid years of living with Jesus and at least seventy disciples. He had heard Jesus's teachings, seen his miracles, and been baffled by his parables. In one day he had been blessed as a "rock" and thrust behind as "Satan." He knew that Jesus was the Messiah, the Christ of God. He was an eyewitness to countless proofs. But he had not yet put all the pieces of the puzzle together. He still did not understand why the King of kings and Lord of lords had to die on a cross as a despised criminal. Still, Jesus confronted him with the question, "Do you love me more than these?" In effect, he was asking, "Do I have the highest priority and loyalty in your life? Despite your doubts, am I still number one?"

This was not a rhetorical question. It demanded a thoughtful, soul-searching reply. Peter was there when Jesus said, "If anyone comes to Me and does not hate his father and mother, wife and children, brothers and sisters, yes, and his own life also, he cannot be My disciple. And whoever does not bear his cross and come after Me cannot be My disciple .... So likewise, whoever of you does not forsake all that he has cannot be My disciple" (Luke 14:26, NKJV).

Notice that Jesus uses the words *anyone* and *whoever* in these teachings, signifying that the requirement is not for Peter alone but for every Christian who would walk with Jesus in loving service as his student and faithful servant. Discipleship is not for the faint of heart. It never has been and never will be. The battle for truth has been a bloody one, and many a martyr has laid down his life for his Lord. The faint of heart and faith will not stand in the battle (cf. Ephesians 6:12–18).

Beloved, no one can meet the standards above without a genuine agape love for Jesus Christ and a born-again understanding of the worldwide stakes in this battle. Through it all, it is love that motivates Christ's followers to take the risks and to proclaim the gospel with mercy, truth, and courage to every tribe and nation, to peoples great and small, to all who have been created in the image of God for his glory.

No other motivation, natural or supernatural gifting, or work of charity is acceptable or capable of bringing lasting fruit and glory to God. Works of charity and excellent, well- intentioned instruction do not motivate a person to change his worldview. Only the genuine demonstration of the rivers of agape love flowing selflessly to others is able to do that. Note what Paul, through the Spirit, says about this:

> Though I speak with the tongues of men and of angels, but have not love, I have become sounding brass or a clanging cymbal. And though I have the gift of prophecy, and understand all mysteries and all knowledge, and though I have all faith, so that I could remove mountains, but have not love, I am nothing. And though I bestow all my goods to feed the poor, and though I give my body to be burned, but have not love, it profits me nothing.
>
> 1 CORINTHIANS 13:1–3 (NKJV)

Love is precisely why Jesus succeeded in having victory over Satan, sin, and death. His love for his Father gave him the heart to obey in all circumstances and overcome every temptation. People witnessed his impartial justice, his righteous instruction, his humble demeanor, his incredible courage, his perfect love, and the miraculous results. And people wanted it. They still want it.

The best news is this: it is still available. It is not available on our terms, but on his. He knows what works. Most of us are still trying to muddle through with the wisdom of man rather than the righteousness and power and love of God. Love works, and it is absolutely necessary for every successful ministry. And every believer has a ministry! None is exempted, superfluous, or an afterthought of God. Peter, by the Spirit, puts it this way:

> You also, as living stones, are being built up a spiritual house, a holy priesthood, to offer up spiritual sacrifices acceptable to God through Jesus Christ.... But you are a chosen generation, a royal priesthood, a

> holy nation, His own special people, that you may proclaim the praises of Him who called you out of darkness into His marvelous light.
>
> 1 PETER 2:5, 9 (NKJV)

This means that we, brothers and sisters in Christ, are part of God's royal, holy, and chosen nation. We are his unique solution for the evils in the world. We are not asked to give generously and make sacrifices for God. We are asked to love as he loved. Consider what Jesus gave up to be a witness to man and what he did to spread the gospel. When we can do the same as faithful servants, we will truly understand why love is the bond of perfection (Colossians 3:14).

# Conclusion

Beloved of the Lord, the world and the church stand at a crossroads. Technological advances, political experimentations, economic theories, philosophical diversity, and a plethora of religious persuasions have failed to bring mankind to the harmony, peace, prosperity, and love requisite for peaceful coexistence. Since each people group feels its ideas and culture are superior to others, and they either want to impose their views on others or selfishly retreat into a prideful isolation, the world has continued to reel under the wicked schemes of the selfish, proud, and powerful. Since most either refuse to accept an authority higher than man or create a higher authority in their own image, few will accept truth as an absolute. Pride refuses to accept any truth outside of one supporting one's own ideas or prejudices. It's easy, therefore, to understand why God hates pride and why he claims to be the truth. It's also easy to understand why we're in the dilemma that now faces the world.

Furthermore, besides these enemies without, we also struggle with the enemies within. Our sinful nature rebels against the shackles of righteousness, and our self-love recoils at the attribution of any guilt engendered by lustful or lawless behavior. We rationalize our sinfulness, and our darkened minds reject even the possibility that God in us could so modify our behavior and attitudes that we could actually live in righteousness and holiness all the days of our life (Luke 1:74–75).

Beloved, God has the answer to man's dilemma and his problems of credulity. That answer is revealed by the scriptures, Jesus Christ, and the Holy Spirit. That answer is for man to walk in God-given perfection: to walk as Jesus walked here on earth (1 John 2:6). The purposes of God in Christ, the purposes of God in his Holy Spirit, and the purposes of God in man clearly reveal this plan. Will man be able to wade through the swamp of deceptions and lies in order to realize this, accept it, and embrace it? Will the church even accept it and embrace it?

The answers to these questions depend on our response to the trumpet being blown. The warning has been sounded by many, and God's purposes have been revealed. I believe that God is saying again, this time to Christendom:

> If My people who are called by My name will humble themselves, and pray and seek My face, and turn from their wicked ways, then I will hear from heaven, and will forgive their sin and heal their land.
>
> 2 Chronicles 7:14 (NKJV)

The promises are beautiful, and God has repeatedly delayed or cancelled judgment upon sincerely repentant people. But if we will not do these things, then the book of Revelation reveals clearly not only the state of the Laodicean church but also the eschatological events of the times we are entering. Jesus himself said, "Enter by the narrow gate; for wide is the gate and broad is the way that leads to destruction, and there are many who go in by it. Because narrow is the gate and difficult is the way which leads to life, and there are few who find it" (Matthew 7:13–14, NKJV).

Nevertheless, for those of us who will humble ourselves, who will diligently investigate the history, claims, and life of Christ, who will seek and embrace the love and truth of God as revealed by the Scriptures, Jesus Christ, and the Holy Spirit, there will be the joy of understanding and the full assurance of hope that comes through rebirth in Christ. Further, to the ecstasy of the faithful and the surprise of the dubious, they will find that kingdom principles really do work!

At the risk of closing with a "prosperity gospel" or fleshly motivator, let me acknowledge that behavior is often modified by positive reinforcement of desired conduct or by negative consequences to improper actions. While we all ought to do what is right simply because it is right, many of us operate on a more devious or pragmatic level. We want to know the answer to "Why should I?" or "What's in it for me?" or simply "Prove it." "Don't just tell me it works. Show me that it works."

As most of you know, the Bible is filled with illustrations of the blessings that follow obedience and the curses that follow disobedience. Consider the lives of Noah, Abraham, Isaac, Jacob, David, Solomon, Rehoboam, Ahab, Manasseh (son of Hezekiah), and the other kings of Israel and Judah. But if you'd like a study a little closer to home, consider the following history of two families recorded by Bennie Mostert in his book *Against the Tide: Take the Gospel to the Ends of the Earth.*

> The following tale compares the lives of two men and the effect that their lives had on other people and society at large. The one went against the tide, against his old, sinful nature and started living in accordance with the truth of the Word. He established an intimate relationship between himself and God. The other went with the tide, surrendered himself to his sinful desires, instincts and passions, and lived a life without God.
>
> The latter man, Max Dukes, was an atheist and denied the existence of God. He lived an ungodly life and did exactly as he pleased, giving free rein to his every desire. He married an ungodly woman. Of their descendants 310 died paupers, 150 were criminals, seven were

murderers, 100 were alcoholics and more than half of the women were prostitutes. His 540 descendants cost the state US$1.25 million.

The first man, Jonathan Edwards, was converted at the age of twelve and chose to live his life to the glory of God. He lived at the same time as Max Dukes, but married a God-fearing woman. Research indicates that up to the present time there are 1,394 descendants of Jonathan Edwards. Among his descendants there are 13 college presidents, 65 professors, three United States senators, 30 judges, 100 lawyers, 60 doctors, 75 officers in the army and navy, 100 preachers and missionaries, 60 prominent writers, one vice president of the USA, 80 civil servants and public relations officers, and 295 graduates, of whom several became governors of different states in the USA. His descendants did not cost the government a penny, but they did make a tremendous positive contribution to improving others' lives.

One man can make a difference. One man who walks with God will always make a difference. The mustard seed that was planted in Jonathan Edwards's heart grew into a big tree, and many people found shelter, life, and peace in its shadow."[1]

May God grant that we would be among those who, like Jonathan Edwards, choose to walk as he walked and embrace the kingdom of God. And may our lives also bring Christ's love and truth to this hungry world. Christian perfection really is the key, and it really does make a difference. Amen.

# Postscript for Those with Ministerial Gifts

For those of you who have been called by God and given a specific spiritual gift of apostle, prophet, evangelist, pastor, or teacher (Ephesians 4:11), I would like to add a few additional thoughts. God has given us a tremendous responsibility to faithfully proclaim the truth of his word without partiality, hypocrisy, omission, or addition. He wants us to speak his truth in love and to warn those who will not heed his will. One of the passages of scripture that has deeply influenced me in this latter area is from Ezekiel 33. I would like to share it with you here:

> So you, son of man: I have made you a watchman for the house of Israel; therefore you shall hear a word from My mouth and warn them for Me. When I say to the wicked, "O wicked man, you shall surely die!" and you do not speak to warn the wicked from his way, that wicked man shall die in his iniquity; but his blood I will require at your hand. Nevertheless if you warn the wicked to turn from his way, and he does not turn from his way, he shall die in his iniquity; but you have delivered your soul. Therefore you, O son of man, say to the house of Israel: Thus you say, "If our transgressions and our sins lie upon us, and we pine away in them, how can we then live?" Say to them: "As I live," says the Lord GOD, "I have no pleasure in the death

> of the wicked, but that the wicked turn from his way and live. Turn, turn from your evil ways! For why should you die, O house of Israel?" Therefore you, O son of man, say to the children of your people: "The righteousness of the righteous man shall not deliver him in the day of his transgression; as for the wickedness of the wicked, he shall not fall because of it in the day that he turns from his wickedness; nor shall the righteous be able to live because of his righteousness in the day that he sins." When I say to the righteous that he shall surely live, but he trusts in his own righteousness and commits iniquity, none of his righteous works shall be remembered; but because of the iniquity that he has committed, he shall die. Again, when I say to the wicked, "You shall surely die," if he turns from his sin and does what is lawful and right, if the wicked restores the pledge, gives back what he has stolen, and walks in the statutes of life without committing iniquity, he shall surely live; he shall not die. None of his sins which he has committed shall be remembered against him; he has done what is lawful and right; he shall surely live.
>
> Ezekiel 33:7–16 (NKJV)

Beloved, if we're called and gifted by God with a ministerial gift, then we too are watchmen in the church. It is our responsibility to raise the bar to the vision and standards of God as expressed in Matthew 5:48, Ephesians 4:13, and 1 John 2:6, and to sound the alarm when sin invades the church. It is time to bring holiness and righteousness back into the church as standard behavior. We must now acknowledge Jesus's commandment to be perfect as the normative expectation for every Christian, on earth as it is in heaven.

Beware of settling for anything less. Let us not be accused, as the prophets and priests of Israel were in Jeremiah, Hosea, and Revelation:

> Because from the least of them even to the greatest of them, Everyone is given to covetousness; And from the prophet even to the priest, Everyone deals falsely. They have also healed the hurt of My people

slightly, Saying, "Peace, peace!" When there is no peace. Were they ashamed when they had committed abomination? No! They were not at all ashamed; Nor did they know how to blush. Therefore they shall fall among those who fall; At the time I punish them, "They shall be cast down," says the LORD. Thus says the LORD: "Stand in the ways and see, And ask for the old paths, where the good way is, And walk in it; Then you will find rest for your souls. But they said, 'We will not walk in it.' Also, I set watchmen over you, saying, 'Listen to the sound of the trumpet!' But they said, 'We will not listen.' Therefore hear, you nations, And know, O congregation, what is among them. Hear, O earth! Behold, I will certainly bring calamity on this people—The fruit of their thoughts, Because they have not heeded My words, Nor My law, but rejected it."

Jeremiah 6:13–19 (NKJV)

My people are destroyed for lack of knowledge. Because you have rejected knowledge, I also will reject you from being priest for Me; Because you have forgotten the law of your God, I also will forget your children.

Hosea 4:6 (NKJV)

And to the angel [pastor/priest] of the church of the Laodiceans write, "These things says the Amen, the Faithful and True Witness, the Beginning of the creation of God: 'I know your works, that you are neither cold nor hot. I could wish you were cold or hot. So then, because you are lukewarm, and neither cold nor hot, I will vomit you out of My mouth. Because you say, 'I am rich, have become wealthy, and have need of nothing—and do not know that you are wretched, miserable, poor, blind, and naked—I counsel you to buy from Me gold refined in the fire, that you may be rich; and white garments, that you may be clothed, that the shame of your nakedness may not be revealed; and anoint your eyes with eye salve, that you may see. As many as I love, I rebuke and chasten. Therefore be zealous and repent."

Revelation 3:14–19 (NKJV)

We are truly blessed to serve the one true God. He is perfect in all his ways, and as the only creation made in his image, his expectation through Christ and his Holy Spirit is that we also would walk as he walked on earth, perfect in all our ways.

Some of you will say or think in your hearts, "Well, how about you? Are you perfect? Do you claim that you are walking as he walked? Is this some kind of guilt trip you're trying to heap on the church? Why are you upsetting the apple cart and writing these things?"

Some of you would say or think worse, and I understand your feelings. But these are not the right questions or emotions. The real questions are as follows:

1. Has God really commanded us to be perfect? (Matthew 5:48, etc.)
2. Have the finished work of Jesus Christ on the cross and his Holy Spirit in our lives provided a way for us to be perfect? (Romans 8:2–4; 1 John 2:6, etc.)
3. Does man have the ability to appropriate God's provisions for perfection? (John 1:12–13; Luke 11:13; 1 Corinthians 10:13; etc.)
4. Is perfection imputed without behavioral evidence, i.e., righteousness and holiness, or is it demonstrated by it? (1 John 2:4–6; Matthew 7:21; James 2:17–20; etc.)

I have tried to show that the biblical evidence gives strong affirmative answers to the first three of these questions and that James was right about faith without works being dead in the fourth. If I have rightly divided the Word of God and captured his heart for his church in this book, and if walking as Christ walked really has been abandoned as the legitimate and attainable goal of each and every believer, then let's look to Jesus, let's make him our example, let's raise the bar, let's pick up the abandoned key, and let's make way for a revival that will touch and change the church and the world as God intended.

As for me, I've written the things that have challenged me to go deeper with the Lord and the things that, as a fellow watchman, I could not repress. I've heard a trumpet in my heart, and woe unto me if I do not sound the alarm and exhort to action. This book is now in the hands of the Lord and his people. May God bless you as you continue to serve him as watchmen.

# Appendix

## Outline of God's Provision for Perfection

I would like to succinctly review the two-part program that God has revealed to man, which enables and empowers him to live the righteous and holy life he has intended him to live since the beginning.

## Part 1: God's Plan for Jesus Christ

- Visit man as a man to walk with him and exemplify how a life could be lived without sin, even under stress.
- Break man's bondage to sin by redeeming him at the cross. His sinless blood was to be shed to pay for our sins. Life would be given for life, because the wages of sin is death, and without the shedding of blood there is no remission of sins.
- Reconcile man to God. Sin separates man from God, but the shed blood of Christ atoned for our sins and brought us back into personal relationship with him.
- Save all believers from their enemies and from the hand of all who hate them, i.e., Satan, sin, and death.

- Fulfill all the promises and prophecies God had made concerning the first advent of the Messiah.
- Identify and confirm God's new covenant with man: "I will write my laws on their hearts and in their minds." "I'll remember their sins no more." "I will give them a new heart and a new Spirit .... I will put my Spirit within them and cause them to walk in My statutes and they will keep My ordnances and do them."
- Preach the parameters and priority of the imminent Kingdom of God in every city and village.
- Establish his divinity and authority by his life, his signs and wonders, his testimony, his death, his resurrection from the dead, his miraculous appearances afterward to more than five hundred people, and his sending of the Holy Spirit at Pentecost.

## Part 2: God's Plan for His Holy Spirit

- Empower believers to live a righteous life by imparting
    - a new baptism (a washing and filling that takes away the old and makes all things new).
    - a new power over temptation.
    - a new power over sin.
    - a new power to do the same things that Jesus did, and even greater things, here on earth (cf. John 14:12).
- Gift man with
    - a new heart: warm, soft, and alive.
    - a new Spirit: the Holy Spirit of Jesus Christ.
    - a new mind: the mind of Christ.
    - new fruits: love, joy, peace, patience, kindness, goodness, faithfulness, gentleness, and self-control.
    - at least one new supernatural spiritual gift.

  - Teach believers all things and bring to their remembrance everything that Jesus said.
- Glorify the Son and proclaim his deity.
- Guide believers into all truth.
- Intercede for believers in accordance with the will of God.

I urge the reader to review the above again and meditate on the meticulous lengths to which God has gone to rectify the behavioral deficiencies of man reflected in the Old Testament and to empower him to walk in righteousness and holiness all the days of his life, even in this present age. His plan to save and bless mankind is nothing short of pure genius and pure love expressed. Only a doting Almighty Father could have imagined and implemented such a wonderful plan. By thus dealing with both man's sin and his sinful nature and establishing a righteous kingdom both within and without, God has removed every obstacle to righteous and harmonious living for all, a condition mankind has sought in vain to establish without God for millennia.

# Notes

**Preface**

1. Audrey Barrick, "Study: Christian Divorce Rate Identical To National Average," *The Christian Post*, April 4, 2008. http://www.christianpost.com/news/study-christian-divorce-rate-identical-to-national-average-31815/

**The Purposes of God in Christ**

1. Kurt Aland et al. eds., *The Greek New Testament, 3rd ed. (corrected)*, (Stuttgart, Biblia-Druck GmbH, 1985), 283.
2. W. E. Vine, *Vine's Expository Dictionary of New Testament Words*, (Peabody, MA.: Hendrickson Publishers, n.d.), 81–82.

**The Purposes of God in the Holy Spirit**

1. Figgis, John Neville, and Reginald Vere Laurence, eds., "Letter to Mandell Creighton (5 April 1887)," *Historical Essays and Studies, by John Emerich Edward Dalberg-Acton* (1907), Appendix, p. 504. http://en.wikiquote.org/wiki/John_Dalberg-Acton,_1st_Baron_Acton
2. James Strong, *The New Strong's Exhaustive Concordance of the Bible* (Nashville, TN: Thomas Nelson, 1990) #4160, 59.
3. Ibid., #4238, 60. n.b. comment on #4160 above.
4. Aland et al. *The Greek New Testament*, 818.

5. Ibid.
6. *BibleWorks 4* (Big Fork, MT: Hermeneutika™), 2000.
7. Joe Saltzman, "Lying as America's pastime," *USA Today Magazine*, Vol. 135, Nbr. 2734, July 2006.


**The Purposes of God in Man**


1. Edwin H. Palmer, *The Five Points of Calvinism* (Grand Rapids, MI.: Baker Book House, 1987), 100–101.
2. Aland et al., *The Greek New Testament*, 330.
3. Robert E. Kofahl and Kelly L. Segraves, *The Creation Explanation* (Wheaton, IL.: Harold Shaw, 1975), 101.
4. Richard B. Bliss, *Origins: Creation or Evolution* (El Cajon: Master Books, 1988), 21.
5. Randy L. Wysong, *The Creation-Evolution Controversy* (Midland, MI: Inquiry Press,1987), 75–76.
6. Walter T. Brown, Jr., *In the Beginning: Compelling Evidence for Creation and the Flood, 8th ed.*, (Phoenix, AZ: Center for Scientific Creation, 2008), 5.
7. James A. Richards, Francis W. Sears, M. Russel Wehr, and Mark W. Zemansky, *Modern University Physics* (Reading, MA: Addison Wesley Publishing Company, Inc., 1960), 344.
8. Aland et al., *The Greek New Testament*, 821.
9. David Barton, *The Myth of Separation* (Aledo, TX: WallBuilder Press. 1989), 91.
10. Ibid., 91–92.
11. Strong, *Exhaustive Concordance*, 352.
12. C. I. Scofield, *The New Scofield Study Bible* (New York, NY: Oxford University Press, 1967), 1353.
13. Aland et al., *The Greek New Testament*, 779.
14. Strong, *Exhaustive Concordance*, #1374, 24.
15. Vine, *Vine's Expository Dictionary*, 229.

## Perfection: The Abandoned Key

1. Strong, *Exhaustive Concordance*, #5046, 71.
2. Aland et al., *The Greek New Testament*, 414.

## Conclusion

1. Bennie Mostert, *Against the Tide Take the Gospel to the Ends of the Earth*, (Vereeniging, South Africa: Christian Art Publishers, 2002), 16–17

# Bibliography


Aland, Kurt, Mathew Black, Carlo M. Martini, Bruce M. Metzger, and Alan Wikgren, eds. *The Greek New Testament*, Stuttgart: Biblia-Druck GmbH, 1985.

Barrick, Audrey. "Study: Christian Divorce Rate Identical To National Average," *The Christian Post*, April 4, 2008.

Barton, David. *The Myth of Separation*, Aledo: WallBuilder Press, 1989.

*BibleWorks 4*, Big Fork, MT: Hermeneutika™, 2000.

Bliss, Richard B. *Origins: Creation or Evolution*, El Cajon: Master Books, 1988.

Brown, Walter T., Jr. *In the Beginning: Compelling Evidence for Creation and the Flood, 8th ed.*, Phoenix: Center for Scientific Creation, 2008.

Figgis, John Neville, and Reginald Vere Laurence, eds. *Historical Essays and Studies, by John Emerich Edward Dalberg-Acton*, 1907.

Kofahl, Robert E. and Kelly L. Segraves, *The Creation Explanation*, Wheaton: Harold Shaw Publishers, 1975.

Mostert, Bennie. *Against the Tide: Take the Gospel to the Ends of the Earth*, Vereeniging, South Africa: Christian Art Publishers, 2002

Palmer, Edwin H. *The Five Points of Calvinism*, Grand Rapids: Baker Book House, 1987.

Richards et al. *Modern University Physics*, Reading: Addison Wesley Publishing Company, Inc., 1960.

Scofield, C. I. *The New Scofield Study Bible*, New York: Oxford University Press, 1967.

Strong, James. *The New Strong's Exhaustive Concordance of the Bible*, Nashville: Thomas Nelson, Inc., 1990.

Vine, W.E. *Vine's Expository Dictionary of New Testament Words*, Peabody: Hendrickson Publishers, n.d.

Wysong, Randy L. *The Creation-Evolution Controversy*, Midland: Inquiry Press, 1987.

www.ingramcontent.com/pod-product-compliance
Ingram Content Group UK Ltd.
Pitfield, Milton Keynes, MK11 3LW, UK
UKHW020137250325
456668UK00001B/59

9 781595 543530